The Louisville Slugger®
Complete Book of Women's
Fast-Pitch Softball

by
John Monteleone and Deborah Crisfield

photography by Michael Plunkett

A MOUNTAIN LION BOOK

An Owl Book

Henry Holt and Company

New York

Henry Holt and Company, Inc.
Publishers since 1866
115 West 18th Street
New York, New York 10011

Henry Holt® is a registered trademark
of Henry Holt and Company, Inc.
Louisville Slugger® is a registered trademark of
Hillerich & Bradsby Co., Louisville, KY

Copyright © 1999 by Mountain Lion, Inc.
All rights reserved
Published in Canada by Fitzhenry & Whiteside, Ltd.,
195 Allstate Parkway, Markham, Ontario L3R 4T8

Library of Congress Cataloging-in-Publication Data are available.

Henry Holt books are available for special promotions and premiums.
For details contact: Director, Special Markets.

Designed by Max Crandall

Printed in the United States of America
All first editions are printed on acid-free paper. ∞

10 9 8 7 6 5 4 3 2 1

CONTENTS

DEDICATION

To Jay and Cori, my two little sluggers at home. — D.C.

ACKNOWLEDGMENTS

First and foremost, I'd like to thank the very tolerant Mark Gola at Mountain Lion, plus Randy Voorhees, Joan Mohan and, of course, John Monteleone. I am also forever grateful to the coaches, trainers, and players who allowed me to pump them for expert information: Mike Candrea, Tricia Carrol, Cindy Cohen, Ken Erickson, Marc Hill, Bob Jones, Jennifer McFalls, Jay Miller, Rhonda Revelle, Shelly Stokes, Ralph Weekly, and Teresa Wilson.

Mountain Lion, Inc. would like to give special thanks to those who assisted in shaping the pages of this book. David Sobel, senior editor for Owl Books, and assistant editor Anne Geiger, for their editorial guidance and eternal patience.

Bill Williams of Hillerich and Bradsby, who gave his full support into getting this project off the ground.

Michael Plunkett, photographer, who took all the high speed, stop-action, and step-by-step instructional photographs.

Margaret Trejo of Trejo Production, who meticulously constructed the pages of the book.

Max Crandall, who designed the pages to make them easily accessible to the reader.

William Drennan, copyeditor, Eileen Delaney, proofreader, Deborah Patton, indexer, and Joanna Bruno, salesperson at AP Wide World Photos.

We would also like to thank Rider University softball players Danielle Lake, Kim Merkel, and Heather Sonnenburg for their modeling services and technical advice. Hopewell Valley Central High School athletic director Steve Timko for use of his field and model softball players Tara Allen, Kelly Cramp, Emily Rizza, and Kim Scheese. Future softball stars Stacia Nero and NaKeya Campbell for their assistance in the Getting Started section, and another special thanks to Princeton University softball head coach Cindy Cohen and Rider University softball head coach Tricia Carrol.

Photo credits: All photographs were taken by Mike Plunkett and John Monteleone except for images from AP WideWorld Photos, which appear on pages 3, 52, 93, 129, 138, 149, 151, 166, 172, 184, and 186.

INTRODUCTION

Softball made its debut in November 1887 as an indoor version of baseball, appeasing a group of Yale and Harvard alumni who were looking for a diversion on an unpleasant, wintry day. The score of the first game was 41–40, and the players used a tied-up boxing glove as the ball.

Over a hundred years later—thanks to refined rules and vastly improved equipment—the sport has exploded in popularity. Softball moved outdoors and has taken the country by storm, attracting more than 40 million players. If you include both slow pitch and fast pitch, softball is the number one team sport in the United States for both men and women.

This book is about fast-pitch softball, the version of the sport found in most women's high school and college programs, and more recently, in the Olympics. The 1996 summer Olympics in Atlanta gave us the debut of the sport, and Team USA did not disappoint, bringing home the gold. This is hardly surprising, however, given that the United States has won six of the last eight World Championships.

Every aspect of fast-pitch softball is covered in this book. The first section is on the offensive game, covering the basic hitting skills, vision training, situational hitting—such as bunting, slapping, and hitting strategy—and baserunning. The second section is devoted to defensive play. It covers the basics behind catching, fielding, and throwing, the various defensive positions and their responsibilities, and defensive strategies. The third section covers pitching, both its fundamentals and the advanced pitches. It also details the fielding responsibilities of a pitcher, a pitcher's training routine, and pitching strategies. The fourth and final section covers strength and conditioning. Olympic players and coaches around the country have contributed their knowledge and advice to create the most comprehensive coverage of softball possible. The book should appeal to both coaches and players at all levels of the game.

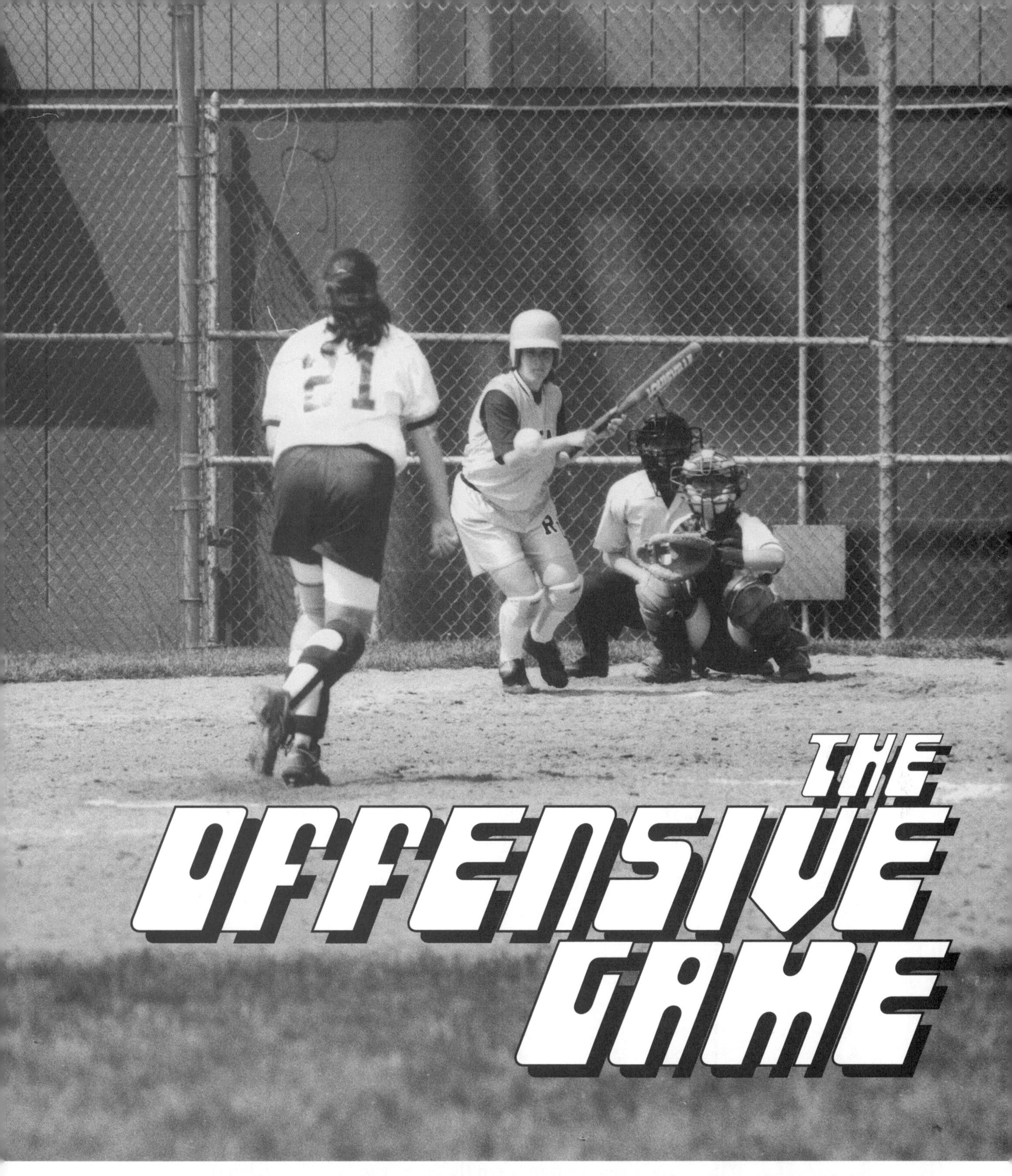

THE OFFENSIVE GAME

TPS Louisville Slugger®

LOUISVILLE POWERIZED

-10

MODEL FP1 · MADE IN USA · MICRO THIN WALL · 29 INCH 19 OUNCE (-10)

THE FUNDAMENTALS OF HITTING

Hitting is the most difficult act in all of sports.

H itting is certainly the most difficult thing I've ever tried to do." So spoke basketball superstar Michael Jordan after he had quit his sport to try his hand at baseball. Imagine his reaction if he had stepped into a batter's box in a women's fast-pitch softball game, where the pitcher is a lot closer to the batter. When Olympic pitcher Lisa Fernandez challenged major-league All-Star player David Justice, she struck him out three times.

The top women pitchers in softball throw the ball more than seventy miles per hour. The ball travels the very short distance of forty feet from pitcher's mound to the plate. A hitter has a split second not only to decide whether to swing at the pitch, but then to actually make contact with this speeding, spinning, darting sphere. This is a skill that takes an extraordinary amount of practice to perfect. There are very few top-notch hitters. With work, though, you can be one of them.

However, before you can step up to the plate, you must prepare. For starters, you need to find a bat that feels comfortable. Then you need to learn the proper grip and develop the basic fundamentals of the swing: stance, stride, rotation, swing, and follow-through. Mastering this takes countless hours of practice and repetition. There are no shortcuts to becoming a good hitter. With hard work, however, your comfort level and confidence will increase in the batter's box. Ultimately you'll be counting down the minutes leading to your next at-bat.

CHOOSE YOUR WEAPON

Bats come in a variety of shapes, sizes, weights, and materials. It can be confusing to a beginning player. When your coach dumps a bag of seven or eight bats against the backstop, where do you begin? Will you get more power from the additional mass of a heavier bat? Or will a lighter bat allow you to snap your wrists more quickly and propel the barrel (the cylinder-shaped hitting area above the handle or grip) faster? Do you want a shorter bat or a longer one? The longer barrel will give you more hitting surface, but a shorter barrel will increase your bat speed. Generally, as players get better, they can opt for shorter barrels, because they are consistently hitting the ball in the same spot on the bat.

Use your body as a guideline when first choosing a bat. While standing, place the bat at your side and let your arms hang loose. If the knob near the handle of the bat is at your palm or lower, the bat is probably too short. If it is higher than the wrist, it is probably on the long side. Essentially, one that hits you right at wrist level is a good bat to start with. Then you can experiment from there.

Select a bat that is the correct length and weight and that feels comfortable in your hands.

Let me tell you. This is a hitter's game. You need to be putting some time into hitting. If you are scoring six or seven runs a game, you are not going to lose too many games.

—Ralph Weekly, coach of the U.S. national team and head coach, University of Tennessee, Chattanooga

BAT SPEED VS. BAT MASS

Many coaches instruct their hitters on the importance of bat speed, which is simply the speed of the barrel of the bat as it passes over the plate—that is, through the hitting or ball-contact zone. A heavier bat can increase power, but to reach maximum power you have to be able to sufficiently accelerate the barrel of the bat into the ball. So make sure the bat you use is light enough to generate proper swing speed.

If you are strong enough to handle a heavier bat without sacrificing balance and form and without significantly diminishing your bat speed, go ahead. *A heavier bat swung at the same speed as a lighter one will increase the flight distance of a fly ball.* To

Softball legend Dot Richardson celebrates after hitting a home run during the 1996 Olympic Games in Atlanta.

An athlete should select a bat that is the heaviest weight she can swing without losing bat speed or mechanics of the swing. For example, I use a 33-inch, 25-ounce bat because when I swing a bat that's even one ounce heavier I lose bat speed and form.

—Dot Richardson, player, U.S. Olympic team

achieve optimum power and consistency, swing the heaviest that you can handle. This will put to work for you the two most important power factors: speed and mass (or weight).

After you have settled on a weight, you should experiment with bats of varying length and barrel size to see what feels best with your swing. Barrel size considerations include the circumference and the size of the sweet spot. The circumference is the distance around the barrel of the bat at its thickest point. The sweet spot is the point or area of the barrel that gives you the most energy exchange into the ball. If you hit the ball elsewhere on the bat, you will waste energy by absorbing too much of it. This cuts down on distance and sometimes results in "stinging" of the hands.

Here is how to find the sweet spot of your bat. Grab the bat at the knob and hold it fairly loosely and then tap it with another bat. The point where you get a totally different sound and no vibration in your fingers is the sweet spot of the bat. Mark it with a piece of tape. This is the ideal spot to strike the ball.

If you own your own bat—one that is properly fitted—you can take additional batting practice when your team is not practicing. And by spending hours swinging your bat, including continually hefting and gripping it, you will improve your chance of success in the batter's box. Heft your bat when you're watching television, swing it in your backyard, or swing it in front of a mirror to get a sense of what your swing looks like.

Swinging your bat in front of a mirror is one of the best ways to train your muscles to remember what they should be doing on each swing. Japanese baseball teams have installed mirrors in their clubhouses for their players to practice their swings, and some major-league baseball teams use portable mirrors alongside their batting cages in spring training. Once your muscles are trained to remember the exact movements of a good, fundamental swing (this is called muscle memory), then your mind can focus on the pitch. The more comfortable you feel with your weapon, the more confidence you will take into each at-bat.

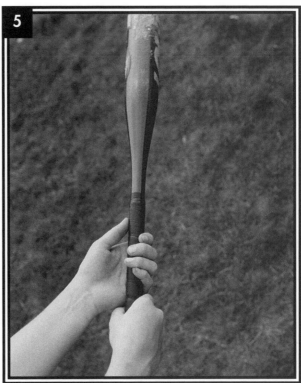

Lay the bat across your hand where the bottom of the fingers meet the top of your palm (4). Wrap your fingers around the handle to grip the bat. Grip the bat only tightly enough to control it (5).

LEARNING TO GRIP THE BAT

Now that you have found your bat, you must learn how to hold it. If you are right-handed, your right hand goes on top, and if you are left-handed, your left hand does. The bat is held primarily by the fingers, not in the palm. Many young players mistakenly hold the bat in their palm down by the thumb, but remember that the fingers are going to do the work. You can start the grip by putting the bat right at the spot on your hand where the fingers meet the palm. Then close your hands around the handle.

Make sure your hands are together, as any space between them will cause you to lose power, and then check to see how your knuckles line up. There are three sets of knuckles in your hand. The first are the knuckles near your fingertips. The second set is in the middle of your fingers, and the third is near the bottom of your fingers. To grip the bat properly, the second set of knuckles from your top hand should line up between the second and third set of knuckles in your bottom hand. Technically, they should line up a bit closer to the second set. You hold that grip all the way through the swing.

Some players skew that grip a bit, lining up the second knuckles of the top hand with the third knuckles of the bottom. This will bury the handle of the bat in the palm of the top hand, which is wrong. If you hold it in the palms, you will lose bat speed and power.

HITTER'S TIP

Holding the bat with your fingers is critical. You have considerably more strength and control with your fingers rather than your palm. As a test, try holding the bat in your palm and have someone try to yank it out of your hand. They can probably do it, can't they? Then hold the bat with your fingers. Now you are able to hold on to it.

Grip the bat so that the middle knuckles of your top hand align with the area between the middle and bottom knuckles of your bottom hand (6). Choking up on the bat, that is, gripping it higher on the handle, will improve bat control (7).

The best way to get used to a proper grip is to swing the bat time and time again. Practice swings (or dry swings) allow the hitter to focus on nothing but the swing itself. With no ball or pitch to worry about, there is no concern over making contact. Dry swings are excellent for working on fundamentals such as the proper grip. Once the hitter feels comfortable with her grip swinging the bat, hit some balls off a tee to become familiar with the feel of the grip while making contact.

WHERE TO GRIP THE BAT

Where you hold the bat on the handle is a matter of preference. Many players like to hold the bat down by the knob at the end of the bat. Others feel more comfortable with a grip that is higher up on the handle. Some hitters may hold the bat a quarter inch above the knob, while others hold it as high as three inches above the knob. This is called "choking up" on the bat. Hitters often choke up on the bat for reasons other than comfort (which will be discussed later in this section), but when finding your personal grip, comfort is the only concern.

Whenever you pick up a bat, make sure your grip is correct, but keep it loose by "milking" the grip—that is, by lifting your fingers rhythmically in succession until the pitcher begins her motion. This will keep tension out of your grip. Tension (gripping the bat too tight) will reduce bat speed and diminish power in your swing. Always maintain a relaxed grip on the bat, much like holding a pencil. Do not worry about the bat slipping out of your hands. Once you start your swing, your fingers will tighten up on the handle naturally as you make contact.

THE STANCE

Your stance is the base for your swing. It gives you support and balance, neither of which you can do without. There are no hard-and-fast rules telling a player how to stand in the batter's box. Each player on the softball team might have a different stance, yet all of them might be successful. Some players adopt different stances depending on the situation. Others find a stance that works for them and then stick with it. Regardless of personal preferences, however, your main goal is to be balanced with your weight centered over your body. As Cindy Cohen, the Princeton University coach, says, "Your shoulders are over your hips, and your hips are over your knees."

The stance is the foundation of your swing, so it's important that you find a comfortable one to work with. The best advice for young hitters is to use the most basic stance possible. This allows the hitter to make the transition from the stance to the swing quickly and without much effort.

Stand with your feet spread slightly beyond shoulder-width with good knee flex. Your arms should be up and away from your body with both eyes facing directly at the pitcher.

In a basic stance, the feet should be shoulder-width apart. This will give you good balance. The knees should be slightly bent or flexed, with your weight on the balls of your feet. This puts you in the "athletic position." As an athlete, you may be familiar with this position from competing in various sports. When playing defense in basketball or football, waiting for a serve in tennis, or playing goalkeeper in soccer, players use this position as a base. It is the perfect foundation for a hitter as well.

Place your weight on the balls of your feet. To test whether your weight is properly distributed, try lifting your heels up while you are in your stance. If you cannot lift your heels, then your weight is too far back toward the heels. Be careful about shifting too far forward, however, because if you are up on your toes, you will be falling over forward. Have a coach or teammate lightly push you from the front (at your sternum) and then from the back side (between your shoulder blades). If you struggle to keep your balance from either side, your weight is not adequately set on the balls of your feet.

This is a closed stance, with the hitter's front foot closer to home plate than her back foot (9). In the square stance, the front and back foot are equidistant from home plate (10). In an open stance the hitter's back foot is closer to home plate than her front foot (11).

You have to be adaptable. It depends on where the pitcher is throwing you. If the pitcher is a predominantly inside pitcher, obviously you are going to have to open up your stance slightly or move away from the plate slightly, but I want to emphasize slightly. You do not want to make major changes or shifts in your basic hitting approach.

—Ken Erickson, head coach, University of South Florida

The batter's box in women's fast-pitch softball is three feet wide by seven feet long. That's a lot of area to choose from when taking your stance. Again, personal comfort is critical, but there is a basic location to begin from. Generally, it is best to line up your back foot with the back corner of the plate. Because the pitch will be judged as a strike or a ball *when it crosses the plate*, being aligned with the plate will help you judge the pitch better. Good judgment of the strike zone helps to avoid swinging at bad pitches. If you stand back farther in the box, for example, you might find yourself swinging at pitches that drop out of the strike zone.

Some other players, however, such as the Olympic team's Michele Smith, prefer to stand in the back of the box no matter what. It gives them a fraction of a second longer to read the pitches and react. Moving back in the box might be a good adjustment when facing a pitcher who throws an exceptionally good fastball. Sometimes all a player needs to get out of a slump is the knowledge that she has made a change that will make her hitting easier. If you are struggling with the bat, your position in the box may be something to consider adjusting.

Whether you are standing near the front of the batter's box or toward the back, always make sure you have full plate coverage. This means that when your arms are extended and your striding foot has touched down, the barrel of the bat covers both the inside and the outside part of the plate. You may have seen players tap some part of the plate (sometimes it is the outside edge, sometimes it is the middle of the plate) before bringing the bat into the ready position of his or her stance. This lets them know that they are the right distance away. But do not move in so close that the pitcher can pitch you inside and force you to make contact with the ball before you can extend your arms, and thus strike the ball below the barrel of the bat (get jammed!). *Your reach with the end of the barrel should not go beyond the outside edge of the plate.*

A hitter with a short, compact swing should stand closer to the plate. Someone with a longer swing who needs to get her arms extended out over the plate should move off the plate. Pay attention to your results as well. If you are struggling with outside strikes or inside strikes, you may be able to improve simply by adjusting your location in the box.

Let's assume that you have found your spot in the box. How do you align your feet? Do you place them parallel to each other (a square stance), place the front foot closer to the plate (a closed stance), or place it farther away from the plate (an open stance)?

The open stance gives you a better view of the pitcher. It is good for players who are slower getting their hips around or for any players who are facing an exceptionally fast pitcher. It positions you well for inside pitches, but leaves you vulnerable for outside pitches. The closed stance will allow you to handle the outside pitches better and hit to the opposite field. It does make you susceptible, however, to the inside pitch. So, as you can see, opened and closed stances can have both positive and negative influences on your success as a hitter.

Finally, make sure the dirt in the batter's box is even under your feet. This may not seem important at first, but think about it. If you are standing in a hole (back foot *lower* than the front foot) or on a clump of dirt (perhaps putting your back foot *higher* than your front foot), your body can lose balance and stability. And during the swing you will rotate your hips and shoulders at an angle (not parallel to the ground). Loss of balance, instability, and uneven rotation all can increase the difficulty in meeting the ball squarely. It might not seem like much, but when you are trying to hit a lightning-fast pitch, every detail counts.

I might move in the box depending on what the pitcher is throwing. If she's a dropball pitcher, I'm going to move up. If she's a riseball pitcher, I would stay back. I might shorten my swing if I'm having problems.

*—Shelly Stokes, player,
U.S. Olympic team*

BAT POSITION

Where you hold your bat when you take your stance is a matter of personal preference, but beginners can follow the general guideline of resting the bat on the shoulder and then lifting it up slightly. Your arms should be in an upside-down V. Coaches may try to advise a specific bat position for you, but more than anything, you want your bat to be in a relaxed position.

The best advice for young hitters is to hold their bat close to where their swing begins. This avoids any exaggerated movements in getting to the point where you start your swing. The less movement you have leading up to the swing, the easier it will be to time the pitch. Timing the pitch simply means having the barrel of the bat make contact with the pitch as it enters the hitting zone. If your swing is too early or too late, your timing is off.

If a batter is successful, I do not mess with her bat position. I had a great hitter who started with her hands way up and then she moved them and did all these things, but when the pitch was released, she was in the same position as everyone else.

*—Cindy Cohen, head
coach, Princeton University*

Rest the bat on your shoulder and then raise it into position as the pitcher begins her windup. This helps you remain relaxed until the moment of truth.

The more movement you have as a hitter, the more movement you have to time, so it is easy for a pitcher to disturb your timing with a change-up, for instance. The first thing to check is the stride. Make sure it is a very short, soft stride. That's your timing element.

—Mike Candrea, head coach, University of Arizona

THE STRIDE

The stride is the small step a hitter takes just before she swings. It is the trigger for getting the upper and the lower body into the swing and the incoming pitch. The stride is a natural movement, just like the small step a player takes when she throws a ball. It is a very simple component to the swing, but it must be executed correctly to achieve success as a hitter.

The stride is a timing mechanism that places the hitter in a balanced position. It is not an aggressive or a bold forward movement. The stride should be a small, light movement of the front foot directly toward the pitcher. On average, most players like to step about six inches, but it can vary, depending on the hitter. On one end of the spectrum, some players merely like to lift the foot up and place it down in the exact same spot, but others like to stride almost a foot.

Your hitting stride will be quite unlike the step you might take if you were going to walk out to the pitcher's mound. When you step forward or stride to hit, your weight should not immediately go forward with the step—that is, do not *automatically or simultaneously* roll your weight onto the front foot. Keep 90 percent of your weight on your back foot and on the inside of your back leg until you commit to your swing. If you shift your weight too soon you will prematurely open your hips and move the top of your body over your front leg as well as diminish the rotational speed of your hips, shoulders and arms. The result is a devastating loss of bat speed and thus hitting power.

So the step forward will be more like the step you would take on thin ice, tapping the surface but not totally committing your weight. This is extremely important, because the stride happens in the decision-making stage, and you do not want to be committed to swinging if the pitch is bad. Even when you don't swing (take the pitch), you still take your stride as the pitch is released. In taking a pitch you stride, but then disengage the lower body's aggressive transfer of weight and all the sequential elements of the swing.

Although the type of stance (open, closed, square) a hitter uses is optional, the direction of the stride is not. No matter how your feet are aligned in the stance, the stride should always go directly back at the pitcher. You also do not want to stride toward or away from the plate. The stride doesn't vary according to the location of the pitch—that is, a player should not step toward the plate for an outside pitch. To begin with, there isn't enough time to see the pitch, take the stride, and then swing. You also need to remember that you have already made sure that your bat covers the entire plate. If the pitch is on the outside corner, you can reach it without stepping toward it, and if it is farther out, you should not be swinging at it anyway. The stride should be the same small step toward the pitcher every time. It is the trigger that sets the swing in motion. Remember, the stride is a very simple step in the hitting process. If not done correctly, however, it can be devastating to the swing.

Three common faults of the stride are termed "stepping in the bucket," "overstriding," and "lunging."

Stepping in the bucket is when the hitter steps away from the pitch. Instead of striding directly back at the pitcher, a right-handed hitter steps toward the shortstop, and a left-handed hitter steps toward the second baseman. This decreases a hitter's plate coverage, making her vulnerable to outside strikes. Stepping in the bucket is common among young hitters who are afraid of being hit by the pitch.

Overstriding occurs when the hitter simply strides too far. When the legs are spread too far apart, the head and the eyes drop, and tracking the movement of the pitch becomes more diffi-

14

A firm, solid base is the mark of a good hitter. Keep your hands and weight back as long as possible so that you can explode into the ball.

The lower body is a great foundation and a great base, but any time that you overuse it or overrotate it, it is going to take the hands and the body away from the hitting zone. What we do is create a stationary base. We try to land in the same place every time with the front foot. We try to keep the forward body motion as still and quiet as we can.

—Ken Erickson

This hitter's poor striding technique (too much toward home plate) did not allow her to fully rotate her hips. The result is reduced bat speed and diminished power.

cult. Striding too far also inhibits the full rotation of the hips, which ultimately decreases bat speed and increases the batter's vulnerability to inside strikes.

Lunging is when the hitter's weight lurches totally or partially onto the striding foot before the batter commits to swinging. Remember, the majority of your weight is supposed to stay on your back leg when you stride. Lunging negatively affects the hitter's timing and vision. The head moves forward, making it difficult to judge the speed, location, and type of pitch being thrown. Lunging also makes it difficult to move the barrel of the bat through the hitting zone with proper speed (because hip rotational movement is decreased), and it makes it nearly impossible to make a level swing.

THE LAUNCH POSITION

At the same time that the foot is striding, your arms are going to move slightly back, just an inch or two, to stretch muscles. This is called the launch position. This is the position from which you will start your swing. It is important that the hands move slightly back to the launch position before they come forward. Imagine the backswing of a soccer player kicking a soccer ball, a hockey player taking a slapshot, a tennis player hitting a ground stroke, or a pitcher preparing to throw a ball. In each of these, there is backward movement before exploding forward to strike or throw the object. This helps generate maximum power. The softball swing is no different.

TEACHER'S TIP

Beginners often have trouble with the launch position. They understand the stride and the weight shift, but the slight coil with the hands is often left out. It seems to be a difficult concept for them to grasp.

If you have a player with this problem, here is a tip that might help her recognize the motion. Have the player try to hit something she knows is going to be much heavier than the softball—a swing tire, for example. She will automatically come back a little before her swing. Her brain knows subconsciously that she has to gear up a little to get that tire to move. Stop her just as she is about to swing. Hold the bat and ask her if she felt what she did. Repeat this several times until she understands the launch position. If you need to, videotape her before and after so she can actually see the movement and the difference.

THE PIVOT

The pivot begins with the transfer of weight from the back leg to the front leg or striding foot. Push off the back leg and open the front hip, rotating the back hip so your belly button faces the pitcher on contact with the ball. In pushing off of the back foot, think of this as "squishing the bug out." This image helps to convey the force needed in this motion. If you like the bug imagery, just picture driving that bug several feet into the ground.

Upon completion of the pivot, your back leg will form an L, and your hip rotation will continue to nearly 180 degrees (it must go at least 90 degrees). Your rear heel will be pointing straight up in the sky, and the toe of your back foot will be pointing directly toward the pitcher.

Full rotation of the hips allows you to harness maximum power from both the lower and upper parts of your body. This is the swing of a power hitter.

16

ROTATIONAL DRILL

If you are having trouble incorporating the hip rotation into your swing, this drill is a good one for you. Place the bat behind your back at your hip area. Hold it in place with your hands. Have your coach soft toss a pitch to you and try to hit the ball swinging with your hips rather than your hands. Make sure it is a quick motion. You can even do this without the ball, just to get a feel for how your hips need to rotate quickly and how your feet pivot hard on the ground.

At this point your weight is transferred over the center of your body. What keeps the weight over the center of your body is a stiff front leg. The lead foot should stay pointed toward the plate and the leg should be firm. If the front leg is bent, your weight will shift out in front of your body, and you will lose balance and power. The pivot allows your hips to rotate toward the pitcher. Hip rotation increases bat speed and adds power to your swing.

During the rotation, your arms still have not moved, except, of course, for the slight movement backward into the launch position. Keep them compact and in an upside-down V, so at the next part of the swing, when you go out after that ball, you get full extension and therefore full power.

THE SWING

You are aiming for a tension-free, relaxed, yet forceful swing. To minimize tension, pay attention to how you think about hitting the ball. Many players want to hit the ball *hard*, and they want to *kill* it. When players are thinking *hard* or *kill*, they tend to tense up with their hands and upper body, which throws off their swing, slows down the bat, and decreases their power.

They grip the bat so hard it causes what is termed "white knuckles." This is a deadly flaw. It needlessly contracts and tires the muscles—especially the upper and lower arms—when they should be in a semiresting state, relaxed but ready to engage when the brain sends the signal to react to the pitch. One way to avoid the onset of "white knuckles"—and thus to relieve body tension—is to "milk" the grip (methodically lift and drop your fingers) as you await the windup and delivery.

Another way is to visualize a quick, reactive swing rather than hitting the ball *hard* or *killing* it (*crushing* it, if you will), which invariably translates into a longer (you only need an extra split second to miss a pitch), less effective swing. Picture your hands behind you resting on a shelf (the launching position), eyes attentive to the pitcher's delivery. Keep your hands relaxed but poised to whip the bat through the hitting zone in the shortest route to the ball at the latest possible moment. Imagine the bat meeting the ball just as your wrists square the barrel to the ball's path, not a moment sooner or later. Throughout, think *meet the ball* or *smack the ball*, not *crush the ball*.

When a player removes thoughts of overpowering the ball, she tends to wait till the proper moment to commit her hips, shoulders, arms, and hands (packaged in that order, please). Once committed, bring your package as quickly as you can. Don't overswing or "muscle" the ball—this slows and/or lengthens the swing. It can also tilt (away from parallel to the ground) the plane of your hip rotation and thus move your head sideward rather than slightly forward and down.

Once you have made the commitment to move from the

As the hands move out of the launch position and the swing nears the moment of truth, the knob of the bat should point at the ball. Also, note how the hitter bends her legs to allow her body to get into a position to hit a low strike (17). As you make contact, the wrists should remain unhinged to achieve maximum extension and power. Premature hinging of the wrists, called rolling, reduces power and most often results in pulling the ball on the ground (18).

launch position and go for the pitch, you must—above all—make contact with the ball. As you pivot on the back foot, the first movement with the hands should be to pull the bat slightly down and toward the pitcher. You should literally point the knob of the bat at the ball. Be careful not to drop your back shoulder. Bringing the bat down is done with the hands, not your shoulder. Just before you make contact, your hips should be facing forward (remember, belly button looking at the pitcher). At this point the path of your swing should be on a level plane, with your wrists still unbroken.

Then-snap!-your arms are fully extended as the elbows and the wrists whip the bat at the ball. Ideally you want your arms and the bat to form a straight line at or slightly after contact. If you swing without making full extension of your arms, you will

HITTER'S TIP

Saw the knob off of one end of an old wooden bat. Then, when no one else is nearby, take a swing at the plate, letting go of the bat at the point where you think you would be hitting a strike down the middle of the plate. If you have used proper extension and hand motion, the bat should go sailing straight up the middle toward the pitcher. If it does not, then you know that this is a problem area in your swing. If you are a right-handed batter and the bat flies out toward left field, then you know the top hand is dominating your swing. Your wrists are probably rolling over before you make contact with the ball. If it flies to the right side, your bottom hand is pulling too long through the hitting zone and you're snapping your wrists too late.

Roll the top hand over after contact to allow for a full follow-through.

Big muscles do not play an important role in the swing. The fast-twitch small muscles that are in the forearms and the fingertips and the hands are the ones that you want to utilize the most.

—*Ken Erickson*

lose quite a bit of power. If you are fooled by an off-speed pitch and your arms are fully extended before you make contact with the ball, keep your top hand from rolling over. This will enable you to lift or "serve" the ball over the infield. If a pitch is too far inside to get your arms extended, pull them in toward the body and rotate as fast as you can—you can often turn this adjustment into a softer, shorter line drive into your power alley or down the line.

As you make contact, your weight shifts onto your front foot. Keep your knee slightly bent on that front leg. The weight shift from back to front and the contact of the bat with the ball should happen at the same time.

As the bat connects with the ball, your top hand will be palm up toward the sky and your bottom hand will be palm down. Then, just after contact is made, roll your wrists over so the top hand is palm down. The top hand should work hard to snap the barrel of the bat into the pitch, but the wrist should not actually roll over until after contact is made. Rolling the wrists over is crucial to a strong follow-through, but it is the snap of the bat that a lot of coaches refer to that generates bat speed and power. What you are really doing is accelerating the head of the bat at the moment of impact. When you begin your hip and shoulder rotations, it is the bottom hand that pulls the bat to the plate, but the top hand is the hand that provides the power to whip the bat across the plate.

A common swing fault is to roll the wrists too soon. When this occurs, the hitter expends power. If you notice you're pulling a lot of ground balls or hitting balls in the air with topspin, the wrists are rolling at or before contact. Keep in mind that the wrists snap to thrust the barrel of the bat into impact, but they don't roll until after contact is made. This will allow you to hit the ball harder and farther, and into the air with backspin.

If you are having trouble grasping the different roles each hand plays, try batting one-handed. Make your normal swing with the bottom hand. Feel how it pulls the bat. Then do a swing with the top hand. You should feel more power from this one as it pushes and whips the bat through the swing.

Your arms should be fully extended at the moment of or just after contact, and the swing should be on a slightly downward

Never cut your swing short. In a full follow-though, the bat will finish behind you.

arc. This will allow you to hit good, solid line drives and ground balls, not to mention allowing you to use gravity in your favor. An uppercut will almost always result in a fly ball, and unless you connect perfectly every time (and how likely is that?), you will not have the strength to get it over the fence. It is an easy out.

During this whole time, keep your head as still as possible. Your eyes need to track the ball, and excessive head and eye movements make this difficult. Finally, you want to follow through. You are going to continue to pull the bat around past the point of contact, and come all the way behind yourself. Your bat should end up near the middle of your back. Some follow-throughs may look different than others. It depends on the type of hitter you are and the swing you own. Regardless, every hitter *must* follow through to complete the swing. Young hitters commonly stop their swing just after contact is made. This is another error, which results in a loss of power. Without a follow-through, that sharp ground ball you hit through the infield for a single now becomes an easy ground ball for an infielder.

Players have different hitting styles. Some are power hitters, such as Olympic outfielder Kim Maher. Others are spray hitters, such as the Olympic catcher Shelly Stokes. They may not do everything exactly the same way or look the same when they hit. You may differ as well. The object is not to hit a specific way just because it works for the best hitter on your team. The goal is to find what works best for you.

The female athlete tends to have less upper-body strength, and hitting is a skill that evolves from the elbows down. The less strength they have, the more upper body they try to use, which can cause a lot of problems. So we try to do a lot of work with the hand action to make sure the hands always stay inside the ball and that we're going to unwind from the bottom up. If you know anything about kinetics, that's basically the strongest movement you can have as a hitter. The bottom half starts, the hands lag, and finally the hands explode through the zone, and the last thing that explodes is the barrel.

—Mike Candrea

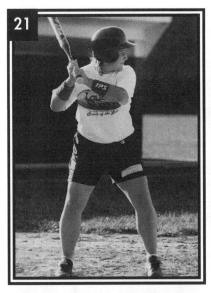

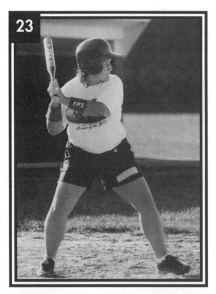

Starting from a comfortable stance, take a short stride and push your hands back into the launch position (23). Pull the bat down toward the hitting zone (24 and 25), pointing the knob of the bat at the ball. Your back foot will pivot (26), opening your hips and allowing the bat to accelerate through the hitting zone. At contact (27) your wrists remain locked in the "palm up, palm down" position. Roll your wrists over after contact (29) and follow through strongly by finishing with the bat on your back shoulder.

FIXING THE FLAWS

Do not abandon the sport if you cannot immediately figure out what is wrong with your swing. It is difficult. Think about it: If all it took was a quick read through an instructional manual, then coaches would lose their jobs, and we would all be Olympic prospects hitting well over .300. It is one thing to know what you are supposed to be doing, but it is quite another to figure out which part of your swing is the part that is failing you.

To help you focus your search, here are the fifteen common errors a batter can make, along with the poor hitting results that might follow as a result. Look for a match in the following three lists and you might be able to solve your problem.

GETTING A PIECE OF IT

Analyzing where your ball goes can be a big clue as to where your swing is failing. If you are popping up regularly or finding the ball skipping off the end of the bat, you might want to see if you are making one of these five common errors.

❶ *Stepping in the bucket.* You are missing outside pitches or catching the ball off the end of your bat. If you are connecting with inside pitches or ones down the middle, then you are pulling them foul. Always stride directly back at the pitch.

❷ *Dropping your back shoulder.* You are popping the ball up, because the dropped shoulder is going to force you into an uppercut and to swing under the ball. Keep the shoulder level through the swing and let your hands dictate the path of your swing.

If I want to make a change in a player's swing, the time to do it is in the fall. You do not want to do it in the regular season. If you try to change a player during the spring and she does not have success, they will revert.

—Mike Candrea

❸ *Going for the fences.* Your swing should be a slight downward motion. If you are trying to go for the home run and lift the ball over the fences, you might be unconsciously swinging with an uppercut. Again, if this is your problem, you will pop the ball up or miss it completely.

❹ *Moving your head.* If your head moves excessively with your stride, then it is going to throw your vision off slightly. If you are being fooled on pitches or swinging and missing frequently, this might be your problem. Check your stride because you may be lunging.

❺ *Pulling the bat with the bottom hand.* If your outs are generally weakly hit balls to the opposite field, you may be using too much bottom hand (or lead arm) in your swing. This keeps the barrel from getting through the hitting zone in time to make solid contact. Snap the bat with your top hand as contact is made.

POWER PROBLEMS

Sometimes you connect solidly with the ball but it does not seem to be going anywhere. You have spent time in the weight room, so your muscles are not the problem, but you cannot get that ball to move. The following five batting problems are all going to manifest themselves in a distinct lack of power.

❶ *Big stride.* If you stride too far forward, you will produce a lower-body base (distance between front and back feet) that is too wide. This will result in a slower hip rotation and thus diminished bat speed and power.

❷ *Swinging too hard.* If you take a swing that is too hard, it also tends to be too long, and simply not economical in getting the head of the bat into the path of the ball. This type of swing emphasizes strength rather than timing and quickness and often results in unnecessary preswing tension. Remember, tension ultimately reduces power. Relax your muscles in a preswing routine that concentrates on getting the bat through the hitting zone as fast as possible once you've committed to swinging at the pitch, but not a moment before.

❸ *Lack of full extension.* To transfer all your power to the bat, you must extend your arms fully. Try the exercise mentioned earlier to make sure your arms are going all the way out.

❹ *Weight stays back.* If you do not transfer your weight forward to a point or axis around which you pivot, you cannot deliver the barrel of the bat to a point of contact with the proper speed and consistency.

5 *Rolling the wrists too soon.* If you roll the wrists before contact, you are misdirecting some of your power—that is, you are probably hitting ground balls rather than fly balls. Snap the wrists into and through the swing, but do not roll them over until after contact is made. You want to create backspin (ball carries), not topspin (ball dives to the ground).

TIMING KILLERS

What if you are missing the ball completely? If you cannot notice a lack of power or a foul-ball problem or a pop-up problem, how can you use your at-bats to signal what's wrong? If you are consistently missing the ball, then your timing is probably off. Either that or you need to have your eyes checked. Here are some flaws that affect timing.

1 *Too much movement in stride, drifting, or lunging*—this causes unnecessary movement of the head and eyes (you can't hit what you can't see)

2 *Bat too heavy*—you are late in getting around on the pitch

3 *Bat too light*—you are early in getting around on the pitch (not as common as no. 2)

4 *Stride too long*—no power or pop in your bat because you are way too early in committing to swing

5 *Preliminary bat position is too far from launch position*—you are late in getting the bat through the hitting zone

If you are still having trouble, it's best to have someone videotape you so you can see what is happening. It is very hard to *feel* what you are doing wrong, but when you can see what is happening, you will find it easier to correct the problem. Another tip is to look at the entire swing for a flaw. Do not look only at the part that is obviously wrong. Sometimes an earlier action is forcing you to adapt with another faulty action later.

32

This swing has two major flaws: The stride is away from the pitch and the back shoulder has dropped. This has caused the hitter to drop the barrel of the bat below her hands, an error in technique that will result in a weak pop fly.

33

Make a mental note of each good swing and visualize what you did right as you prepare for each at bat. This will build confidence and help you maintain a positive frame of mind going into each plate appearance.

Once you perfect your swing, practice it constantly. Do not let your body forget what it feels like to take a crack at the ball. Even Olympic players spend hours on their swing. Lisa Fernandez refers to her mirror as her best batting coach. Dot Richardson knew she had to keep swinging, but she had trouble fitting it into her life as a doctor. To save her the commuting time it took to get to the gym, she had a batting cage built in her bedroom. Not all of us have that luxury, but nearly everyone can find a place for a full-length mirror.

ACCENTUATE THE POSITIVE

Hitting is not only a physical act; success at the plate also depends on your attitude when you are there. You need to be confident, relaxed, and focused, which are not as easy as they sound.

There is a lot of pressure at the plate. In many other sports, such as soccer or basketball, someone is frequently right by you to compensate quickly for an error you might make. But, when you step up to the plate in a softball game, the job is yours alone, and you have to make it happen.

Approach each at-bat with a confident attitude. You are better than the pitcher. You are going to get a hit, and there's nothing she can do about it. For some players this self-confidence comes naturally, but for others it takes a lot of work, especially if they have not had a lot of hitting success in the past. The key is to train yourself to think in a positive rather than a negative manner.

Visualization is a technique used by many of the world's greatest athletes. In softball it can be a key ingredient to your success at the plate. While you are in the on-deck circle, think back to a time when you hit a ball right on the nose. Close your eyes, and replay that image over and over in your mind. See the pitch, take the swing, and remember the feel of hitting the softball on the sweet spot of the barrel.

Positive thinking will bring success at a much higher rate rather than negative thoughts. Do not think, "I have to get a hit

Hitting off a tee should be the first step in any hitting instruction if you have the luxury of time and equipment. Technically, until a player can hit the ball off a tee with a fundamentally sound swing, she should not be going against live pitching. The tee removes the variables of pitching and helps a player learn the swing without having to worry about a moving target.

When you have players hit off the tee, make sure they are setting up properly. Generally, players stand too close to the tee and too far up. To know where to stand, they need to get into their full extension to see exactly where they want to make contact with the ball. Draw a line in the ground so they go back to the same spot every time, because the tendency with the tee is to get sloppy and not pay attention to getting a perfect swing every time.

Coaches and instructors often make sure hitters adjust the tee for inside and outside pitches, but often forget to change the height of the tee. Many players just use the tee for that up-the-middle perfect-height pitch, but it is good for all sorts of pitches. They have to learn to hit the harder pitches, because a good pitcher is going to stay away from the middle. By using the tee, the hitter will begin to understand that her swing can't be grooved to specific height to have consistent success. On pitches that are high in the strike zone, the top hand has to work harder to keep the barrel above the ball and hit the ball level. When hitting a low strike, the hitter has to go down with her legs to get the barrel on the same plane as the ball. If she doesn't use her legs, she'll simply drop the barrel with her hands, which will result in pop flies and missed pitches in the game. If she drops the barrel when hitting off the tee, she'll begin to hit the tee instead of the ball.

Once they have mastered the swing off the tee, you can move your players onto the ball machine, adding the variable of the ball in motion. The ball is moving, but it is always in the same spot. Then once they have that down, and only then, move onto live pitching. The minute a player starts doing something that looks wrong or starts slumping or not connecting correctly, then send her back to the tee to fix it. Once she's fixed it, make her swing correctly hundreds of times. The swing should be ingrained in her muscle memory.

Once players start to face live pitching, you do not want them to be thinking about so many things in the batter's box that they are not able to concentrate on the pitch. Coaches often yell last minute hitting instructions such as "Do not take too big a stride" or "Keep your head still," but this is counterproductive. The player has to be concentrating on the pitch. The only thing you want them thinking about is "See the ball. Hit the ball." Fix everything else off of the tee.

here. The team is depending on me. We're going to lose if I do not."
Instead think, "I am going to get a hit." Take the pressure out of
the equation. Focus on the job at hand.

DRILL TIME

STAYING ALIVE

Sometimes batting practice can get a little dull. This drill spices it
up a little. The hitter at the plate stays there only as long as she
gets a bona fide hit. If she hits something that can be fielded
cleanly within the infield, she's out and she moves to first base.
Everyone rotates one position. This drill really teaches the hitters
to focus on placing hits rather than just swinging away. As an
added bonus, it gives the fielders incentive to work hard, so they
get their turn at bat, while at the same time giving them experience at various positions.

FEARSOME FOURSOMES

Another great batting practice drill divides the players into
groups of four. One group of four is up to bat while the rest are in
position out on the field. Players hit, and then run out the ball,
staying on base if they make it. The group of four gets to bat until
each player makes one out. Even if one player is making an out
regularly, she can still be taking batting practice until everyone
else in her foursome makes an out. Chances are that she's the one
who needs the most practice anyway. When a foursome completes
their outs, they replace another foursome on the field. Each foursome should keep track of the runs they score when they are up
to bat.

PEPPER

You can't have a softball book without a pepper drill. Line up four
or five players about fifteen or twenty feet away from a hitter.
One player tosses the ball to the hitter who hits it back with a
half swing. The idea is to have a lot of quick hits at once to   develop eye-hand coordination rather than developing a perfect
swing.

The ball is scooped up by one of the fielders and then tossed
back again. The hitter must hit the ball on the ground to remain

alive. If she hits it in the air and it is caught, then the player who caught it gets to be the hitter. If a player is staying alive for a while, you might want to switch it, so everyone gets a turn.

CALLED SHOTS

Taking batting practice on the field is fun, but it is most productive when each swing you take has a purpose. In game situations, you may be called upon to perform a specific duty with the bat. Practice this and your success rate will improve.

Assuming you get nine swings in a round, lay down a sacrifice bunt for your first swing. On the next pitch, show the bunt, pull the bat back and swing away. The third swing is a hit and run so make sure you hit the ball on the ground. The next two swings are for moving a runner on second over to third base, so hit the ball to the right side of the infield. Next, imagine there is a runner on third base with less than two outs. Look for a pitch you can drive to the outfield. the final three swings are yours. Either practice a situational swing, or just smack the ball hard three times.

Pepper is a great drill for enhancing hand-eye coordination and improving bat control.

TRAINING THE EYES

Have you ever listened to fans at a softball game heckle the umpire? Comments such as "Open your eyes, ump—you're missing a good game," give the impression that the person calling balls and strikes is visually impaired. If vision is so important to the umpire, who is simply calling balls and strikes, you can imagine how important it is to the hitter. All the physical talent in the world is meaningless without possessing vision skills.

Vision, or how well you see the ball, is a vital part of hitting that often doesn't get the attention it deserves.

SEEING THE BALL

When you step into the batter's box, it is time to focus both mentally and visually on the job at hand. You first want to make sure that every thought other than "see the ball, hit the ball" is back in the dugout. Not only do you want to purge the thought of the fight you had with your parents or boyfriend, but you want to get rid of negative softball thoughts, too. The fact that you have gone 0 for 12 the past three games has no place here. You want to be concentrating on this one at-bat, this one pitch. As Olympic catcher Shelly Stokes puts it, "When you step up to that plate, you want to clean house."

A good way to ensure that you are focused at the plate is to have a regular routine that you go through every time you step into the box. For example, you might want to tap the bat on the corner of the plate, dig your back foot in, and take two practice swings. This is your body's signal to your brain that it is time to concentrate on the pitcher and your at-bat. If you practice this routine in nongame situations, you can use the cues of the routine to clear your mind at game time and direct your focus where it should be—on the pitch.

Good hitters are able to block everything out and relax when they step into the batter's box. Some may simply take a deep breath, others focus on looking for a pitch in a specific zone, and some may repeat a little reminder to themselves, such as "Keep your weight back, then explode to the ball."

Whatever your preswing thought may be, you need to direct your attention to the pitcher, and try to avoid being distracted by the movement your peripheral vision may pick up. Now is not the time for you to be noticing your friends in the bleachers. Nonetheless, you do not want to get into a staring contest with the pitcher. You want to focus, but not too intensely. A popular technique is the soft-focus concept. A soft focus is directing your eyes to a broad area such as the pitcher's cap or the letters on her uniform as she stands on the mound. Do not stare at your soft center, but keep your eyes in that general direction. It's important to keep the eyes relaxed to avoid fatigue. Your eyes should keep a

Your eyes should maintain a soft focus (general awareness) on the pitcher during her windup. Look at a spot on the pitcher's shirt or her face (2). As the pitcher prepares to deliver the ball, your eyes should shift to a hard focus. Find her release point and concentrate all your attention on seeing the ball come out of her hand (3).

soft focus until the pitcher begins her windup. As she winds up, your eyes should shift to a hard focus.

A hard focus is a rigid focus on a specific area. That area is the pitcher's release point—simply stated, a pitcher's release spot from which she releases the ball. Once your eyes shift to the release point and pick up the ball, they remain locked on that softball right until the point of contact (assuming you swing). Don't focus on the release point from the beginning because your eyes may get tired if they concentrate on a specific area for too long. This can slightly blur your vision or even cause your eyes to blink. If the eyes blink when the pitch is released or at any time during its flight, your chances of hitting the ball are slim to none. Also, if you focus too soon you will be distracted by the movements of the pitcher's windup, which can upset timing.

Fortunately in fast-pitch softball, the pitcher releases the ball from the same point on practically every pitch, so you know where your eyes have to go on every pitch. A good windmill pitcher releases the ball right at her hip. Do not be distracted by the rest of the arm motion. Zero in on it, and do not let go. In that way your eyes are fresh for the crucial moment and there is no chance of losing focus.

USE YOUR HEAD

Head positioning also plays a big part in your ability to see the ball. If you have a very closed stance, you might not be seeing the pitcher fully with both eyes. Young hitters often tuck their head back in their stance and appear to be peeking at the pitcher with their lead eye (left eye if you're a right-handed hitter, right eye if you're left-handed). This will throw off your depth perception. You have two eyes; you might as well use them both. Make sure your head is turned out, facing the pitcher.

Excessive head movement (as mentioned earlier) harms your hitting ability. If your head is moving, everything is distorted, and your hand-eye coordination is affected. The ball will appear to be moving or bouncing on its path to the plate. It also adds velocity to the pitch. If the pitch is traveling sixty miles per hour and your head is moving forward toward the ball, it gives the illusion that it's traveling more like sixty-four miles per hour.

Finally, watch the ball all the way. Because the ball is traveling so fast, it may seem impossible to actually see the ball hit your bat. However, by trying to track the ball into the bat you will enable your eyes to watch the ball as long as is humanly possible. High-speed, stop-action photography reveals that hitters *do not* track the ball with their eyes all the way to the bat; rather, batters employ superior peripheral vision (vision to the sides), and kinesthetic feel (the sensing of the position of the parts of the body, such as hands and arms, in the swing). Here the hitter *tries to see the ball hit the bat* on every pitch to ensure that her head stays down (thus allowing the eyes to track the ball as far as is

physically possible). Hitters are often so concerned where the ball is going to go when they're about to hit it that they pull their head off the pitch. If this is a habit of yours, the location of the ball will be in the same place every time—the catcher's glove. Don't worry about where the ball goes on contact. You can pick up its location when you take your first few steps out of the batter's box. The object is to connect bat and ball, and if your eyes are looking elsewhere, you are not going to do it.

Even if you're not swinging, discipline yourself to follow the ball all the way into the catcher's glove.

IDENTIFYING THE PITCH

Hitting would not be considered one of the most difficult acts in sports if hitters were challenged with the same pitch time after time. Unfortunately, pitchers became smart enough to realize that speed and location were not enough. Add deception to the mix and you've got a real chess game in the works. Vision is limited not only to seeing the ball, but identifying the type of pitch it is as well. Is it a fastball, a change-up, a drop, a rise, or a curve? Pitch identification is crucial to a hitter's success, and it has to be done in less than half a second.

Though a hitter may panic at first when faced with the daunting task of identifying each and every pitch, there are a whole host of clues that can help. What is the spin on the ball? Does the

Since we've gone to the optic yellow ball with the red seams, it is much easier to pick up rotation on the pitch. When I first started coaching it was very difficult to read the spin of the ball with the white ball with the white seams.

—Mike Candrea, head coach, University of Arizona

pitcher's motion look different? Is her release point different? Is her grip different? Is she slowing down her motion? What is her setup for each pitch? Is it the same or different? These are all things you can look for to help you become a better batter. You should be looking for clues all the time, both in warm-up and as the pitchers are throwing to your teammates at bat before you. Notice the catcher, too, because she might give something away by the way she sets up to catch a certain kind of pitch. If you do notice anything, be sure you share it with the rest of your team, so you can all gain an advantage at the plate. Knowing how to swing the bat is only part of the equation. You also have to know where and when to swing.

Spin Doctor

One way to read the pitch is to zero in on the spin. Focus on the seams and the way they are rotating. This is easier to do in college ball, which now uses yellow balls with red seams. In high school, the white ball with white seams is still the norm, but pitch identification is not quite as important in high school because the pitching is less sophisticated.

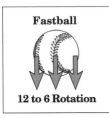

Fastball

12 to 6 Rotation

Fastball: The fastball is the most common pitch. Essentially it is a straight pitch that the pitcher is throwing as fast as she can. It has a straight, forward rotation. The fingers roll straight off the ball and finish pointed up toward the sky. If you think of a clock, the ball is rotating from 12 to 6 (viewed as it heads toward you).

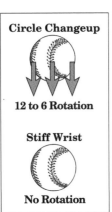

Circle Changeup

12 to 6 Rotation

Stiff Wrist

No Rotation

Change-up: The change-up is a straight pitch that comes in much slower. The easiest change-up to identify is one that is thrown with a stiff wrist. Because the fingers don't roll off the ball during the release, there is no rotation on the ball. If you see seams are not spinning, it is going to be a slower ball. The best change-ups keep the exact same 12-to-6 rotation that a fastball has, which makes them very difficult to detect. The fingers roll off the ball like the fastball, but a lighter grip pressure decreases its rotation and velocity. A good change-up is generally about two-thirds the speed of the fastball: If the fastball is coming in at about sixty miles per hour, then the change-up will be about forty to forty-four miles per hour.

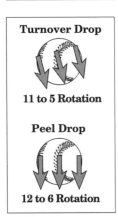

Turnover Drop

11 to 5 Rotation

Peel Drop

12 to 6 Rotation

Drop: There are two types of drop pitches: the peel drop and the turnover drop. Both drop pitches break downward as they cross the plate. Both look like a strike as they are coming in, but the spin will force the pitch downward just as you swing for it. The spin to look for is just like the fastball, a 12-to-6 rotation, but the turnover drop might be tilted slightly on its axis. The best way to identify the peel drop is to look for the pitcher's palm facing downward just before the release, as less white (or yellow) of the ball will be visible. To spot the turnover drop, look to see the hand turning over the top of the ball as it's released.

Rise: The rise breaks upward as it crosses the plate, getting batters to swing under it. This rotation will be backward. Again, with the clock analogy, it will be going from 6 back to 12. This is one of the fastest of the advanced pitches.

Curveball: The curveball spins in a sideways motion and will break right or left, depending on the pitcher. The seams spin sideways, and the pitcher's arm comes across her body on the follow-through.

Knuckleball: This pitch sort of floats in the air, but can have movements in any direction, depending on the wind conditions. This pitch is not commonly used by pitchers because it is simple to identify. The knuckleball, like the stiff-wrist change-up, has no rotation, and the grip (mentioned later in this chapter) is easy to spot.

Picking up these different spins is a skill that comes from lots of experience and good vision. Some players will *always* find it difficult to pick up on spin, but there are drills you can do to help yourself learn. For instance, when a pitcher is practicing her different pitches, step up to the plate with a glove rather than a bat. As you are standing in your batting stance, try to catch the ball backhanded with your glove. Then identify the type of pitch. Not only will this give you extra experience identifying pitches, but it will also help you train your eyes to follow the ball without having to worry about the swing at the same time.

GET A GRIP

Pitchers, by necessity, have to use different grips for different pitches. Most of them try to hide their grip in their glove, but occasionally they get sloppy. Take advantage of a pitcher who shows her grip early, and use it as a tip to what type of pitch is coming.

Rise
6 to 12 Rotation

Curveball
Sideways Spin

Knuckleball
No Rotation

Once you recognize that off-speed pitch, you can't automatically think about pulling it. You have to think up the middle or to the opposite field. If you do try to pull it, your weight will get out in front of the pitch, your top hand will roll over too soon, and you are going to hit a ton of ground balls to the shortstop (or second base if you are a lefty).

—Mike Candrea

TEACHER'S TIP

Ken Ericksen, the head coach at the University of South Florida, has a drill that he thinks really helps his players learn to watch the pitch. This drill allows the hitters to watch the ball for a longer time than they usually get to. Their goal is to hit the ball foul. Right-handers try to hit the ball into the first-base dugout, and left-handers aim for the third-base dugout. In this way they see the pitch as long as possible; which helps them learn what the different pitches look like. It also teaches the batter to wait longer on the pitch to hit to the opposite field.

Take a look at the hand position on the ball when the pitcher is going into the glove and you will be able to see a lot more things than you would think.

—Ken Erickson, head coach, University of South Florida

The windmill pitch is virtually the only pitching motion hitters see in fast-pitch softball today. This works to the hitter's advantage as well. The pitcher's hand comes out of her glove long before she releases it. There is a fair amount of time to pick up the pitcher's grip on the ball. This may tip off her pitches, and here are some grips (Figures 6 through 10) to look for.

Fastball: A three-fingered grip across the seams (Figure 6).

Change-up: If she is throwing the circle change (Figure 5) you will see the thumb and index finger alongside the ball forming a "circle." For the backhanded change, her grip will not be any different from the fastball grip.

Drop: If it is a peel drop (Figure 6), the grip is the same as for the fastball. If it is a turnover drop (Figure 7), the pitcher is going to grip the ball the same but have her fingers on the side of, rather than behind, the ball.

Rise: At lower levels, the rise grip (Figure 6) is the same as the fastball grip, but at a higher level, you might be able to catch the index finger curl (Figure 8). The index finger will curl along the side or up on top of the ball instead of laying alongside the middle and ring fingers.

Knuckleball: A knuckleball (Figure 9) provides the most dramatic grip change. The pitcher will actually grip the ball with the knuckles, forcing it back into the palm.

Stay alert in the box and you may benefit from a careless pitcher showing you her grip on the ball. Knowing what pitch is coming certainly makes hitting easier.

5

This photo caption refers to the batter's stance.

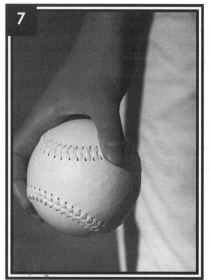

Learn what the grip for each pitch looks like. (6) shows a fastball grip (some pitchers use a similar grip for a change-up). (7) shows the grip for a drop pitch and (8) is a common grip for the rise pitch. (9) is the grip used for a knuckleball and (10) illustrates the grip for a curveball.

Curveball: The curveball grip (Figure 10) is close to a fastball, but the pointer and middle fingers are held together on the ball. The pitcher may also grip slightly to the side.

THE MOTION NOTION

Some pitchers, especially the ones at lower levels, give away their pitch by using a different motion. They slow up, shorten their stride, change their release point, or set up differently on the mound. Make sure you pay attention to the pitcher during warm-ups, when she is throwing to other hitters, and when you are in the on-deck circle. Each pitcher is going to have her own quirks, but here are some common things to look for.

Fastball: Since it's the most common pitch, the fastball is the basis on which you are going to judge the other pitches, so note the setup, speed, stride, and release so you can judge the other pitches by the differences. Pay special attention to the speed of her arm swing.

Change-up: If a pitcher is not careful, she can easily give away her change-up by a change in motion. To begin with, some less experienced players will use a slower motion rather than a different grip. That is the easiest giveaway. Second, if the player is using a backhanded flip for her change, her release will look dramatically different because the back of her hand will be facing you as she flips the ball out with her hand. A stiff-wrist release will also be easy to notice, because there will be no snap. It will appear as if her wrist is locked stiff as she releases the ball.

Knuckleball: The knuckleball also uses a stiff-wrist release. The pitcher looks as if she is almost pushing the ball.

Drop: The biggest giveaway for the drop is the shorter stride so the pitcher can get a greater forward lean of the upper body. This allows her to get the shoulder and arm forward and over top of the ball at release, thus achieving faster topspin. Good pitchers will try to make it as close to the fastball stride as possible, but even they will shorten it a little.

Rise: The riseball pitcher is going to try to lower the center of her body to promote a lower release point of the ball, and you might be able to pick up on that. On the release, she will be rotating her wrist away from the center of her body, as if she is turning a doorknob.

Curveball: The curveball pitcher will stride slightly across her body. Instead of extending straight outward with her lead leg, she will step toward her throwing side. Her arm finishes across her body.

11

Many coaches tell their hitters to "see the ball hit the bat," but in reality, that's not possible. Trying to see the ball hit the bat will help you to follow the pitch all the way in.

KNOWING THE PITCHER

It helps to get to know the pitcher you are facing. Some pitchers give away what they do with their eyes and face. A pitcher may wear a very stern and angry face when psyching herself up to throw a fastball. Others may take a deep breath to relax when throwing a change-up. Often pitchers will look down at their glove

to check their grip when throwing a special pitch, such as a curveball, rise, or drop. Many pitchers have just one other pitch besides the fastball, or maybe two. Very few can throw all types well. Even if this pitcher can, she might have more of a pattern to her pitches than she realizes. After she throws a strike, she always comes in with a curveball, for example. Or if 90 percent of her pitches seem to be fastballs, you can pretty much ignore the rest of them and count on that. Depending on your level of play, this scouting work might already be done for you. If it is not, do what scouting you can during warm-up.

Focus on the release point to pick up the pitch, not the follow-through. Although the pitcher's follow-through varies with each type of pitch, it occurs too late to view it to distinguish what pitch is coming. If you're concentrating on the follow-through, the ball will be past you before you can get the bat off of your shoulder.

EYE EXERCISES

Even if you are not at the level of play where you are able to pick up on rotation (or even need to), training your eyes is still an excellent idea. There are a number of practice drills that will help. For example, you can use a marker and draw large dark numbers on the ball. Then, as you are standing at the plate, try to identify the number when the ball is pitched to you.

Two other ball drills involve someone tossing balls softly at you. The tosser should be down on one knee about five feet away and off to the side. If you are using real softballs, she should also be wearing a catcher's mask to protect her face. Wiffle balls are a good alternative. One way to do the drill is to have two different-colored balls, one red and one blue, for example. Have a soft tosser

Part of the cat-and-mouse game in softball is trying to find pitchers who get sloppy and give pitches away.

—Mike Candrea

throw both to you at the same time and shout out "Red!" or "Blue!" Then try to hit whichever one she called. If you do not have different-colored balls, you can try tossing one high and one low. In this case, the tosser will call "High!" or "Low!"

ZONING IN

Your eyes are doing their job, locating the ball, and identifying the type of pitch. Now your brain has to determine whether the pitch is a strike and whether it is a strike that would be good for you to hit. This is a matter of knowing your zones: the strike zone and your personal hitting zone. The strike zone is what the umpire is going to use to determine whether the pitch is good, and the hitting zone is what you use to determine whether the pitched strike is one you can handle more easily than other strikes. Just remember: After two strikes, the umpire's zone takes precedence, and you must be prepared to swing at all strikes, not just the ones in your favored hitting zone. This is referred to as "protecting the plate."

THE STRIKE ZONE

The strike zone is defined as the area between the armpits and the knees and above home plate. In reality, however, it is slightly smaller. The umpire will probably call strikes on pitches over all corners of the plate, but rarely would she call an armpit-high pitch a strike. Unless she's a low-strike umpire, a pitch at knee level will also probably be called a ball.

Watch the batters before you to see how the umpire calls the pitches. If a lot of players are getting high pitches called strikes, you will know that you are going to have to protect yourself from those high strikes. The same would be true if the umpire seems to be calling strikes on low pitches. An umpire generally maintains a consistent strike zone, and it's important to learn each umpire's preferences as early in the game as possible. Unfortunately, sometimes it takes an at-bat to really learn where an umpire is calling them. If you get a called strike on an absurdly low pitch, do not get angry. Take that lesson and apply it to the next at-bat. If you get that low pitch again, make sure you swing.

Sometimes an umpire's quirks can work for you. The pitcher is going to have to change her pattern as much as you are. Make her work for her strikes. If you know the umpire has a low strike zone, then you may want to lay off pitches above the waist.

Note: On-base percentage is like batting average except you add in the walks and hit-by-pitches. If you have four singles, two walks, and one hit-by-pitch in thirteen plate appearances, your batting average is .400 (four hits in ten at-bats, two walks, and a hit-by-

Are walks as good as a hit? Absolutely. What I like is on-base percentage (percentage of times you reach base per plate appearance). If you can get on base, you can score. If you can score, we can win, so I really do believe that a walk is as good as a hit. I believe that on-base percentage wins games. We do not even talk about batting average.

—Cindy Cohen, head coach, Princeton University

A good swing thought is for you to look for a pitch "below your hands" (14). Any pitch above your hands (15) is out of the strike zone.

pitch). Your on-base percentage, however, is .538 (seven times on base in thirteen plate appearances).

Even though each umpire's strike zone may vary a little, you still should have confidence in your own judgment. You only have a split second to decide whether you're going to swing at the incoming pitch, so you need to have a very good idea if it's a ball or a strike. Hitting a softball is difficult enough without trying to hit pitches out of the strike zone. Make sure it's a good pitch to hit when you put the bat in motion. Keep in mind, when you have fewer than two strikes in the count, that you can afford to be more selective. When you have two strikes against you, however, you better be swinging at anything close to a strike.

If learning the strike zone is giving you trouble, there is a great strike-zone drill that you can do in practice. While the pitcher is practicing, stand at the plate in your stance. Do not swing, but watch every pitch as it flies by. Call them strike, high, low, outside, etc. See if you and the catcher agree. Notice if you are consistently wrong about a particular pitch. You can also have another player chart the pitches for you. When you and she disagree, she can mark where she thinks the ball came in and what you called. Sometimes a visual graph can help point out weaknesses.

The batter's hitting zone consists of pitch locations that she can successfully handle. If you hit high and inside pitches with authority (as shown above), high and inside pitches are part of your hitting zone.

YOUR HITTING ZONE

The next step is learning which pitches you can handle most effectively. You may know the strike zone to perfection, but if you struggle hitting certain strikes, you better get to know your weaknesses quickly. Try to identify where the pitch is when you get your best hits. Remember pitches that will get you to miss or hit feebly. By analyzing these data you can figure out your hitting zone—the area inside the strike zone (and for some people, a little outside the strike zone) that gives you the most success.

Sometimes it is difficult for a player to realize just exactly what type of pitch is best for her. A good drill, similar to the one for learning the strike zone, can help. Have another player stand behind you when you take batting practice. That player should chart the pitch and what happened when you swung. Did you miss? Did you hit a weak ground ball? A pop fly? A home run? A perfect line drive base hit? Find out if there is a pattern to you during your swings in the game as well. That determines your hitting zone.

Once you find out which pitches work best for you, you can try to set yourself up to get those pitches. For instance, if you like inside pitches, then inch in closer to the plate. The pitcher and catcher might think they can jam you inside.

You want to make sure that your hitting zone is not too narrowly defined, however. If you know you can hit low fastballs and you wait for them, you could end up waiting all day or at least until the umpire sends you back to the dugout. You have to make sure your hitting zone encompasses not only the pitches that are best for you, but also the pitches that are decent for you. Be choosy, but make sure you cover enough of the strike zone.

For the same reason, you are also going to have to practice hitting pitches that are outside your hitting zone yet still within the strike zone. Just as you might know the pitcher's weaknesses, so she might know yours. If the pitcher knows you struggle to hit inside pitches, she may target that area every time you step in the batter's box. With fewer than two strikes in the count, you can hold your swing until something better is offered. Once you have two strikes against you, you had better be swinging at anything that comes near the plate, regardless of whether it is good for you.

DRILL TIME

FINGER FLASH

Because the key to picking up a pitch is finding the pitcher's release point, hitters should practice locating that point. In this drill, a hitter will stand at the plate. The pitcher goes into her motion, but she is not holding a softball. Then, at what would be the moment of release, she flashes either one, two, or three fingers. The batter should call out what number she has flashed.

DRY RUN

Sometimes success at the plate is a matter of visualization. Before you go into a game, take lots of dry-run swings, but do more than practice your regular swing in front of a mirror. Go for low balls and high balls. Adjust to get that inside pitch or that outside pitch. Ask another person to call the pitch. In that way you have to react to what they say, just as you would have to react to the ball. If you can see how your body swings with each pitch, without involving a ball, you will have a better image of what you have to do when the ball is in the picture.

Playing a simple game of pepper helps train your vision.

3

SITUATIONAL HITTING

Every at-bat of every inning in each game is going to be different: the number of outs, runs scored, the runners on base, etc. One of the reasons that softball is such a fascinating game is that each of these situations has its own strategy. For instance, if a runner is on first base and it is late in the game, you might be more likely to sacrifice an out and bunt just to advance a runner, whereas early in the game you might have let the hitter swing away to give your team a chance to score multiple runs. There are several ways to get baserunners to cross home plate. How they get there depends on your team's strengths and the game situation.

The situations are endless, and teams that have numerous methods of attacking defenses win a lot of games. In fast-pitch softball, developing a great offense takes more than swinging the bat and making contact. Good teams make things happen by confusing defenses and finding their weaknesses. To earn a spot in the batting order of a successful team you have to learn what it takes to contribute and produce offensively.

There are many different ways to generate offense and any team that can master them all will be difficult to beat.

2

BUNTING

In fast-pitch softball, bunting is a very big part of the game. A bunt is when the batter allows the bat to hit the ball as it's held parallel to the ground, producing a very short hit. There are several different types of bunts, all of which have unique purposes. Bunting and advancing runners without base hits is referred to as manufacturing runs. If the hitters in the lineup seem to be struggling throughout a game and are not producing hits, you might need to manufacture some runs to get something up on the scoreboard. Bunting is essential to this offensive approach.

Bunting is very different from hitting. Hitting is an aggressive act, whereas bunting is subtle and conservative. Unfortunately, many players do not like to bunt. Swinging away is much more gratifying, but there are times when you need to do what is best for the team. Bunting is an effective tactic both for moving baserunners, and in some cases, stealing a base hit.

SACRIFICE BUNT

The sacrifice bunt is the most common type of bunt and is exactly what it sounds like. You sacrifice your turn at bat for the good of the team. This play is used almost exclusively when the team is

The safest and most common method of advancing a baserunner is sacrifice bunting. Every hitter in the lineup should be able to bunt.

Aggressive offensive strategies force your opponent to play faster than what is normal for them. When a team is taken out of its comfort level, its defense is prone to making either mental mistakes or physical errors. In either case, this makes big run-scoring innings for us.

— Eugene Lenti, head coach, DePaul University

The square stance (3) and the pivot stance (4) are the two most common methods of sacrifice bunting. Practice each method and decide which stance works best for you.

The bunt game is the reason my teams are successful. We bunt more than twice as often as the other teams. Our batting average is mediocre, our hits come less frequently, and our home runs are few and far between. But our runs batted in and our runs scored are on par with anybody.

— Patty Gasso, head coach, University of Oklahoma

trying to advance a runner from first base to second base (or second to third) so they are likely to score on a base hit or a fly ball, ground out, wild pitch, error, etc.

When executing a sacrifice bunt, remember that you are not attempting to get a base hit. If the defense is inexperienced and botches the bunt, you might get lucky and get on base, but this is not your purpose. You are up there to move the baserunner to the next base. Knowing that, make sure you give yourself enough time to get into bunting position. It will help you place down a good bunt. It does not matter if the first baseman and the third baseman start charging in before you even bunt the ball. As long as you bunt the ball in the proper area, you'll get the job done.

To bunt, start in your normal batting stance. You might want to move up in the box, however, if you are usually farther back. This gives you a greater chance of bunting the ball in fair territory. Take your normal batting stance and have a clear idea of exactly what you're going to do. Repeat to yourself, "I'm going to get into bunting position, I'm going to bunt a strike, and I'm going to bunt the ball down the first-base line. If it's not a strike, I'm going to let it go."

There are two ways to set up your feet for the bunt: the square stance and the pivot stance. For the square stance, you want to take a step forward with your back foot as the pitcher begins her windup. Place your back foot as close to home plate as possible. Make sure you do not step on the plate while doing this or you will be called out by the umpire when you bunt the ball. Then step to the side with your front foot to widen your base. This puts

To bunt the ball toward first base (5), push the handle of the bat outward toward the pitcher. This angles the barrel of the bat so that it will direct the ball to the right. To bunt toward third base (6), pull the handle of the bat closer to your body and get the barrel out in front of home plate. This creates an angle that directs the ball to the left. Left-handed hitters should reverse these directions.

your body square to the pitcher. Some hitters step away from the plate with the front foot first, and actually replace the original position of the front foot with the back foot. This takes you too far away from home plate, and you will not be able to cover the outside part of the plate.

The pivot method leaves both feet in the same position and just squares the upper body only. Set up as if you are going to hit away and then pivot toward the pitcher on the ball of your back foot. Keep the knees bent and your weight in the center of your stance. The pivot method avoids the "stepping on the plate problem," but the batter must concentrate on making sure her body is square. It is also crucial to move closer to the plate using the pivot method to ensure full plate coverage. If you stand too far from the plate when you pivot, your bat will not reach outside strikes. Whatever bunting method you choose, your primary goal is to get your body square, facing the pitcher.

Now that your feet are in position, you must get the bat into proper position. As mentioned above, the bat must cover the entire plate. Slide your top hand up the bat, at least to where the fat part of the bat begins. This gives you better control of the barrel of the bat. Next, move the bottom hand up to the top of the hand (or grip) of the bat. This shortens the length of the bat, which also improves your control.

Some players who are just learning the bunt are afraid of getting their fingers hit by the ball, and they do not move their hands up on the bat far enough, but this is a huge mistake. If this is your problem, use Wiffle balls to learn the motion. Then move on to tennis balls. When you are completely confident with your skills, use softballs.

The top hand controls the absorption of the pitch and should be merely supporting the bat, not gripping it. Allow the fingertips to do all the work. The fingertips should stay largely behind the bat. Think of pinching the bat with your thumb and forefinger rather than holding it. You are not directing the bat with this hand, so you do not need a tight grip. The bottom hand is going to control the movement. Assuming you are a righty, and you want your bunt down the first-base line, use your bottom hand to push the knob out. If you want it down the third-base line, pull the knob in. Reverse this if you are a lefty.

Your knees should be relaxed and bent. Push your arms out in front of you and flex the elbows slightly. Keep your eyes about eight inches to a foot directly behind the bat, right at bat level, and place your bat at the top of the strike zone. Laying off high pitches now becomes simple. If the ball is above your bat, let it go.

Angle the barrel of the bat slightly upward. The hitter's natural reflex is to drop the barrel slightly as the pitch is delivered. By having the barrel angled upward, the bat becomes parallel to the ground at the point of contact. If the pitch is low, do not lower your bat with your arms; instead, bend your knees. Your legs do nearly all the adjusting when bunting. This keeps the barrel on a flat plane, giving you the best surface for bunting. It also ensures that your eyes stay at the same level as the bat.

BUNT STRIKES

Just because you move into the bunting position does not require you to bunt every pitch. If the pitch is low and out of the strike zone, let it go. It will be called a ball. It is even more important to stay away from high pitches. These are easily popped up in front of the catcher, which can be dangerous. Not only will you fail to advance the runner, but also it can possibly turn into a double play. This is one of the reasons why you hold the bat at the top of the strike zone. It gives you one less thing to think about. A cardinal rule of bunting: only bunt strikes.

When you see a good pitch, bunt it. That is what you are up at the plate for. Your arms should be extended, allowing you to give a little with the pitch to deaden the ball. A successful bunt hits right at the end of the bat. This will just deaden the ball and force it to drop. A trick to learning this motion is to think of the bat as your glove. When you are catching a ball, bring the glove into your body to absorb the shock and the speed. This is the same idea as for the bunt. "Catch" the ball on the end of your bat. If you do not, the ball is going to bounce right back to the pitcher, and there will be a double play. Ideally, you want a slow-rolling dribbler about three feet in from the foul line, going about fifteen feet away from the plate. Do not poke at the ball. You may bunt the ball too hard, pop it up, or miss the pitch.

You still have to put some muscle behind that top hand, however. Do not make it so limp that the ball pushes the bat back so it is practically facing first base (if you are a righty). The bat should meet the ball straight and out in front of the plate.

Do not rush to run out of the batter's box when bunting. Take your time, and lay down a good bunt rather than trying to hit the ball while your body gears up to run. See the ball on the ground before you start to run to first base. Remember, you are not concerned with reaching first base safely. Your number one job is to advance the runner, and it will not help your team if the ball goes foul or pops up for an out.

BUNT STRATEGY

When you look down at the third-base coach and she flashes the bunt sign, it's important that you understand why you're being asked to bunt. It's your at-bat that's being sacrificed, and you should have a clear understanding to how it's helping your team. Comprehending why you're sacrifice bunting will help you realize where to bunt the ball and will also give you more incentive to get the job done. Any time a player is asked to carry out a responsibility, it helps for her to know the reason behind it.

A player on first is a good start to an inning, but a player on second can score on a base hit. Advance a runner to second safely, and you have made a valuable contribution to your team. Understand that a sacrifice bunt is good for the whole team, and although a bunt may not give you individual glory, it may be critical in giving your team an opportunity to win the game.

Sacrifice bunts are valuable at nearly every stage in the game. They are good early in the game, when you want to get that first run on the board. They are good when the game is tied and you want to get ahead. They are good when you are down by a run and you need to tie the game up. Bunting may seem like a boring job, but it is critical when it comes to winning close games.

On the other hand, there are times when you do not want to bunt. If you are down by more than a couple of runs, players should swing away to try to get a big inning. Outs are valuable when you're trailing and you can't afford to give any away.

7

To bunt a low strike (and this is the best pitch to bunt), bend at the knees to lower your body to the ball. This allows the bat to remain on a level plane and brings your eyes closer to the ball.

Players get out in practice and get drilled to death. Grounder, grounder, grounder. Bunt, bunt, bunt. But do they understand why they are doing certain things? They'll be so much better if they know why. Coaches also need to teach strategy.

—Patty Gasso

After we score a runner who was put into scoring position by a bunter, the first person I congratulate is that bunter who sacrificed her at-bat to advance the runner into scoring position.

—Patty Gasso

Even if sacrifice bunts do not play a significant role in your team's strategy, practice them every day. There will be times when you are called on to bunt, and if you have not practiced and mastered the skill, your efforts will likely fail. When you practice bunting, make it gamelike. Try to be accurate and have a purpose in mind each time you square around.

THE PUSH BUNT

The push bunt is a bunt where the batter tries to *push* the ball past the pitcher while keeping it short of the infielders. It is similar in technique to the sacrifice bunt, but it has a different purpose. You're attempting to get a base hit. Instead of moving a runner who is already on base, the push bunt is used to get yourself on first base.

Many players hear the term "push bunt" and reach out with the bat and push. This is not the correct method of execution. Using a pivot stance, extend both arms, letting the ball hit the bat rather than the bat hitting the ball. The trick is not to let the bat "give" with the ball.

Although the push bunt can be used as a sacrifice bunt, it can get you to first base if the situation is right. A good time to attempt a push bunt is when you see that the shortstop and the second baseman are playing deep. The trick here is to bunt the ball hard enough to get it past the pitcher, but soft enough so it's not a routine ground ball. If you're a right-handed hitter, send the push bunt to second base; if you're a lefty, send it to shortstop.

THE DRAG BUNT

The drag bunt, also called the sneaky bunt, is a surprise move where the batter bunts the ball away from the pitcher in an attempt to get a base hit. If you are a fast runner and can learn this skill, you will immediately become dangerous at the plate. In fact, if you are a fast runner, you should make learning the drag bunt a priority.

Many players do not realize the value of the successful drag bunt. Fielders will play up closer in the infield every time you step up to the plate, which opens up holes if you decide to swing away. Just the fear of you laying down a successful bunt will force coaches to adjust their defensive strategies. Any time a team has to adjust their defense takes them out of their game and is an advantage to your offense. A successful drag bunt has the same result as any other single. It looks the same in the stats book. Once you get the hang of it, it may seem easier than getting a hit swinging away.

The key for a drag bunt is waiting until the last second to show the defense what you are doing. Surprise the infield. It is especially effective if the first baseman and the third baseman are playing deep. If you are a right-handed batter, bend your left knee

A left-handed hitter uses a crossover step when executing the drag bunt. The upper body must remain square to the pitch until the ball is bunted. If the shoulders turn toward first base prematurely, the hitter will be unable to bunt pitches over the outside part of the plate.

and drop your right leg back just as you're about to hit the ball. This keeps you from running into the ball, which often occurs when you feel the need to get out of the box too quickly. The drop step back controls your approach and still puts you in running position. You'll be able to push off to run the instant you make contact with the ball. Once the ball is in play, take off!

If you're left-handed, a drag bunt is a little more complicated. Once you perfect it, however, you'll experience great success. Take a small step with your front foot toward first base—which opens the hips. Then, as you go to bunt the ball, come forward with your back foot, crossing it over the front foot while making contact with the ball. At this point you'll already have momentum heading toward first base.

Hold the hands in the same position on the bat that they are in for the sacrifice bunt, but angle the bat upward a bit more. Also, do not extend your arms outward as you do when sacrifice bunting. Hold the bat a bit closer to your body.

Your bottom hand pulls the handle in toward your midsection to bunt the ball down the third-base line if you're right-handed or the first-base line if you're left-handed. Do not chop at the ball; instead, redirect it to produce a soft ground ball. Try to bunt the ball as close to the foul line as possible. The last thing you want is to bunt an easy ground ball back to the pitcher. As soon as the ball hits the bat, you're off and running. Remember, if you are going to miss with your accuracy, make sure you miss foul.

Starting from your regular stance, pivot on your back foot (slightly) to open your hips to the pitcher (10). Pull your arms in toward your midsection and move both hands up on the bat. As the pitch is released, take a crossover step with your back foot and push your arms out to make contact with the ball. Try to time the pitch so that you make contact as your crossover foot lands (11). Bunt the ball near the end of the bat (to deaden the ball) and run to first base.

THE RUN AND BUNT

The run and bunt is a tactical play used to advance the runner from first base to third base. Here is how it works: The runner takes off for second on the pitch. The hitter squares around to bunt the pitch if it is a strike. If it is not a strike, then the runner is on her own and slides into second base for a steal. If the pitch is a strike, the hitter bunts the ball down the third-base line. This placement is important because it will bring the third baseman off her bag to field the bunt, possibly leaving the bag open for the runner. The runner rounds second base, looking to advance to third base. If third base is open and the runner thinks she can make it safely, she never stops running.

HITTER'S TIP

A proper bunt is easier to master than hitting. The problem is that players just do not practice it enough to perfect it. It is a great skill, even for a good hitter, because you never know when you might need it.

Patty Gasso, the head coach at the University of Oklahoma, has always made bunting a large part of her team's practice, and she has found it valuable in situations she did not anticipate. "A while back, I had a left-handed leadoff batter. She was unbelievable. This girl could hit the ball over the fence. She could hit every gap. She could slap. She could sneaky bunt. She could do it all. But then she let the mental part trip her up. She was in a slump and could not hit the ball for anything.

"I finally told her to just start using the sneaky bunt for every at-bat. Well, she started to get on, and her confidence started boosting. Once she knew that she could fall back on the sneaky bunt, she started to swing away again. She was back to being great. So if you have a kid who's slumping, just not hitting the ball at all, have her work on her sneaky bunt to get on."

SUICIDE SQUEEZE

The suicide squeeze is a bunt play that is used when there are fewer than two outs with a runner on third base. It is called a "suicide squeeze" because if the batter does not bunt the ball, the runner has committed suicide. It is an exciting play that is used almost exclusively in the late innings of a close game. The squeeze bunt is not used very often, but its rarity is one of the reasons that it works.

As the pitcher releases the ball, the runner breaks for home while the batter pivots to bunt. The batter must bunt the ball no matter where it is pitched. The runner never hesitates or slows down on her dash for home. Once the ball is bunted fairly, there is no way the defense has time to get the runner at home plate. The squeeze play can really excite your offense, too, while it demoralizes the other team at the same time.

As mentioned earlier, you must bunt whatever pitch is delivered regardless of its location because the runner on third is going home the moment the pitch is released. Even if the pitch is coming at your feet, you must somehow get the bat on the ball. Focus on getting the ball down on the ground, which is always important in a bunt situation, but especially key here. It's even more important than where you place the ball. If you miss, the runner has just committed suicide as the catcher waits, ball in glove, for the runner to reach home.

Pivot into the bunt position just as the pitcher releases the ball. You cannot use the square-around method when you squeeze. It takes too long, and it's important not to show the bunt too early. If you do, the pitcher can alter where she throws the ball. She could pitch the ball out of your reach outside or high, which would be suicidal to the oncoming base runner. As with bunting for a base hit, the element of surprise is a key factor in the squeeze bunt.

I've been known to have runners on second and third and call for the squeeze on the first pitch. Boom. We get the runner home. The defense is reeling and then on the first pitch of the next batter, we do it again. They never dream that we'd do it twice in a row. You want to demoralize another team, do the squeeze on them twice in a row.

—Patty Gasso

14

If properly executed, the suicide squeeze is nearly impossible to defend against.

Where should you bunt the ball? Try to peek at the first baseman and the third baseman. Is the third baseman deep? How about the first baseman? The majority of the squeezes go to the seam on the first-base side, but if the first baseman is way up, then you want to bunt it down the third-base seam. Some coaches even have placement as part of their squeeze signal. If you have a left-handed first baseman and a left-handed pitcher, bunt it between them and you can squeeze all day long. Always pay attention to any weaknesses in the defense.

Some coaches tell their batter to get out of the box slowly, which slows up the catcher. Do not try this in a game. You could be called for interference by the umpire. You (as the hitter) are not allowed to hang around the batter's box after the ball is in play. The last thing you want is a perfectly executed squeeze ruined by attempting to bend the rules.

Another, less effective, option is the safety squeeze. In this version, the runner holds back until she sees the batter bunt the ball. The advantage to this is that the bunter can choose a strike to bunt, instead of possibly having to bunt a high pitch, for instance. The disadvantage is that the runner on third loses quite a bit of her jump, since she has to wait for the batter to bunt the ball.

HIT AND RUN

When a runner is on first base, there is a whole new range of possibilities. You can move the runner over to second base with a sacrifice bunt. A drag bunt could advance the runner and possibly put you on first base. The aggressive approach is to swing the bat to stroke a base hit or an extra-base hit. But swinging away may also result in a force-out at second base, or even worse, a double play. The hit and run is a good way to avoid this scenario.

A hit-and-run play occurs when the baserunner runs on the pitch and the hitter swings the bat to protect the runner (and

On the hit and run play, try to hit the ball on the ground. This hitter does an excellent job of raising her hands to get the barrell of the bat above the ball. She hits the top half of the ball, resulting in a ground ball.

hopefully make contact). The hitter *must* swing at the pitch and should try to hit the ball on the ground. The baserunner must look in to home plate to see if contact is made. If there is no contact, she is on her own to steal second base. If the ball is hit in the air, she must retreat to first base. If the ball is hit on the ground, she should continue running and look to go on to third base.

The success of the hit and run is heavily dependent on the hitter. It works best if the batter is a good contact hitter. Not only does that give greater assurance that the runner will be protected, it also gives a chance of a base hit, which will advance the runner two bases.

Any time you find yourself at the plate in a hit-and-run situation, look to your coach for the sign. *This is a sign you cannot afford to miss.* A good coach will put the hit-and-run sign on only when the count is in the hitter's favor (2 and 1, 2 and 0, 3 and 1). This gives you the best opportunity to see a good pitch.

As mentioned earlier, you must swing at the pitch no matter where it is thrown. Even if the pitch is over your head, you have to swing to protect your teammate on the base paths. If you are fortunate enough to get a good pitch, do your best to hit the ball on the ground. It allows the runner to advance whether you're safe or out. Try to swing down on the pitch to hit the ball on the ground and out of the air. A pop fly is worthless and destroys the play.

Keep in mind that the runner breaks for second when the pitch is released. With the runner in motion, one of the infielders will break to cover second base, leaving a big hole in the infield. A good place hitter will exploit that hole for easy base hits. This is an advanced form of hitting, but a good way to earn a base hit.

The best way to avoid the double play is to make sure you have speed at the plate and speed on the bases, but unfortunately, you can't always have those. So if you work on bat control at the plate, you can execute the hit and run. We look to put out runners in motion more than a lot of other teams. That often keeps you out of the double play.

—Ken Erickson, head coach, University of South Florida

The key to hitting the ball to the outfield is getting a good pitch in your hitting zone. Trying to lift the ball into the air by making changes to your swing is not the proper way to drive the ball to the outfield.

RUN AND HIT

With a fast runner on base, the run and hit may be a better option than the hit and run. In this situation, the runner steals second, but you do not have to swing if the pitch is not to your liking. Having a runner with good speed enables you to execute this play with very little risk. If you do not swing, the runner has a good chance to swipe second base with her speed. If you do get a good pitch to hit, there's that large hole in the infield created by the runner in motion.

SACRIFICE FLY

The goal of the sacrifice fly is to score the runner from third base. Once again, the batter sacrifices her at-bat for the good of the team. She does her best to hit a long fly ball into the outfield. The second that ball is caught, the player on third tags up and takes off for home. With luck, the throw from the outfield will be too far to catch the runner at home and a run will score. Obviously, the sacrifice fly can only be done with fewer than two outs.

When there is a runner on third base and fewer than two outs, you should look for a pitch you can drive to the outfield. Most hitters have an easier time lifting the ball into the air on a pitch up in the strike zone, but some like the pitch low. A good approach is to look early in the count for a pitch you can hit well. If you get it, don't hesitate to rip at it. Do not allow the pitcher to get ahead of you in the count. Take the action to her and be aggressive in run-scoring situations. The last thing you want is to find yourself behind in the count and swinging at the pitcher's best pitch.

SLAP HITTING

The slap is essentially an infield base hit from the left side of the plate. Your goal is to put the ball on the ground into the gaps in the infield and beat out the throw to first. Because the distance to first base is so short—only sixty feet—and because a lefty has an advantage out of the batter's box—she's closer to first base—the slap has proven to be quite successful. Although the hit is fairly new to the women's game, it has been a part of the men's game since the sixties. Men who were familiar with the slap began teaching it to the women, and it has become an integral part of the game's strategy.

One of the great things about the slap game is that it has opened up more opportunities for players to play at the collegiate level. High-school players who had great speed and great athletic ability, but were below-average hitters, did not stand a chance to play softball at the Division I level. Now coaches can put their speed and their eye-hand coordination to good use by having them slap. Time yourself to see if it will work for you. If it takes you about three seconds to get to first, think about learning to slap-hit.

The slap is not a bunt and not a swing. The closest motion to it is a chop. You want to get the barrel of the bat above the ball. Aim for the holes in the infield, either in the direction of the shortstop or the second baseman. The shortstop is generally preferable, because she has a longer throw to first, but if you are playing against a second baseman who is cheating over toward first base (the first baseman has to move in to cover the bunt possibility), then hit the ball to second. Either way you go, you want it to be a soft and slow hit. If they keep the first baseman back because they know you are a slapper, then forget the slap and go with a bunt down the first-base line.

The key to the slap is keeping the hands back when you make contact. Keep your shoulders closed while you open your hips to the pitch. The open hips allow you to move quickly, but the closed

The short game in softball has become a very big weapon, because all you have to do is put the ball on the ground and then explode toward first base. If you have speed, the shortness of the field will allow you to be very successful.

—Mike Candrea, head coach, University of Arizona

TEACHER'S TIP

The person you should make a running slapper is a person who can be convinced that she will never be anything but a running slapper. That will be a hard sell. You need to convince her that it is all about on-base percentage, because if she gets on, we do not care how she got there. Never take a turtle and try to turn her into a slapper. You probably do not even want to do it with an average runner, though you can.

The first time I saw the slap was in 1987, playing Indiana. That same year I had a hitter—or, more accurately, a player who swung the bat—who couldn't hit to save her life. I asked her to get her eyes checked, and she really got mad at me. She was a really good athlete, but she couldn't even hit the pitching machine consistently. She already hit lefty, so I started to think that maybe this would work for her, although she wasn't one of the fastest out there.

For two years that's all we ever let her do. And she was the best, even though she wasn't so fast. Then her junior year we let her hit a little. Then her senior year she was pretty good at it because her eye-hand coordination had really been helped by her slap.

—Cindy Cohen, head coach, Princeton University

Begin your crossover step just as the pitch is released.

If you have a real rabbit, think about telling your slapper to take second, too, because who is covering? Short is fielding the ball. The second baseman is heading to first. Your girl has to be fast and aggressive to try this, but it can be done.

—Cindy Cohen

shoulders keep your hands back. As the pitch comes in, get the bat above the ball, stop, and chop. You want your head to be over the hole your arms make. Key on this. It helps to keep your hands in and aligned with your body. If the hole gets out in front of your head or if you try to hit the ball out in front, you are going to pop it up. It is almost impossible to hit down on the ball if your arms are out in front. Hitting the ball down on the ground is the key element in the slap.

Your hands need to be soft and relaxed when you make contact. This keeps your hits weak off the bat, but still allows you to take a quick swing. If you try to slow your swing down to hit the ball softly, it will affect your timing and you may miss the ball completely. The fact that your hips have already cleared (opened) and your swing is cast in a chopping motion will take enough power out of your bat.

You can also do a hard slap in certain situations. If the middle infielders are counting on you to slap and are coming in and playing you up tight, try a hard slap, because they will not be able to cover as much ground and you are more likely to get the ball through a gap. Some hard surfaces also will give you a high-bouncing chopper, which is difficult to field quickly. If you see a middle infielder moving to cover a base, either a soft or a hard slap is effective. The hard slap will get through the hole they are creating, and the soft slap will dribble through the infield, far away from an available fielder.

To learn the slap motion, start with a tee. The slap is an awkward motion, and you really want to get a feel for the hit before you put the upper half of the swing with the lower half. A lot of players tend to hit the ball foul consistently. Make sure the barrel of your bat is pointed toward fair territory.

Once you have mastered the chopping motion, then you can add the feet. You want to be hitting the ball when the weight of your body is on your left foot because your right foot is opening up toward first. Keep in mind, however, that even though your hips are opening up, you still want your step (or steps) to be directly back to the pitcher. If you fly open to first base, you will never hit an outside pitch (and the other team will figure this out).

Some slappers like to start in the back of the batter's box and then run through it to get their momentum started. This can be very successful unless the slapper wants to bunt or becomes a hitting slapper. In that case she will probably be standing back for the slap and forward for the bunts (or hits), and the surprise element is completely removed.

If you feel comfortable with your footwork after practicing with the tee, you can add a soft tosser, a ball machine, and finally live pitching to your practice routine. Do not expect to become a proficient slapper in the first year. It is a tough skill to master. Once you are doing well, try swinging away occasionally to keep the defense guessing and to make the slap an even greater weapon.

To really throw the defense off, you can fake the bunt and then slap. To do this, you want to pivot into bunt position and slide the top hand only part way up the bat. Because it is not going all the way up the barrel, you have to sell the bunt with your body, which is why you have to pivot. Then you want to bring your bottom hand up to meet the top one at the last second, and as the third baseman and the first baseman are rushing in, you slap it by them. Your hands are choked on the bat quite a bit when executing the fake bunt and slap, giving you better control of the bat.

Move your hands ahead of your body, keeping your wrists firm and the barrel back. The barrel must trail the hands to create the angle necessary to hit to the ball to the left side.

Begin in your normal stance near the back of the batter's box. Pivot slightly on your back foot (22), shift your weight on to your front foot, and then push off your back foot to begin your forward movement toward the pitch (23). Take a crossover step with your back foot directly toward the pitcher, making sure that your hands lead the barrel as you move forward and that the bat is held high in the strike zone (25). Allow the pitch to get back in the hitting zone (27) to enable you to hit the ball to the left side of the infield. Take a short, downward swing keeping your wrists locked through contact (28). As your wrist rolls over, drop the bat and sprint to first base.

DRILL TIME

TARGET BUNTING

Because a good bunt is placed down the third-base line or the first-base line without going foul, you want to practice placement in addition to technique. Line up some bats three feet in from each foul line, marking off the areas where you want the bunt to go. Then get in there and bunt. For every bunt that lands between the bats and the foul line, you get one point. For every ball that lands in the middle, between the two rows of bats, you subtract a point. See if you can end up with a positive score after twenty bunts.

LINE BUNTING

This is a good bunting drill that gives fielders practice in scooping up the bunt at the same time it gives a hitter lots of bunting practice. Line up about five fielders, each with a ball. One player stands at home plate with the bat, and another player stands on first. The first fielder tosses the ball to the bunter, who then bunts it down either line. The tosser must field her ball and throw it to first. She then gets her ball back and goes to the end of the line. Meanwhile, the next player has already tossed her ball to the bunter, and so on and so on. Players should rotate through the tossing line two or three times, and then the next player becomes the bunter, and the former bunter joins the tossing line. You can set up a few "home plates" and "first bases" to have everyone doing this at once.

THE ART OF BASERUNNING

As a player sprints around the bases, seldom do you hear a spectator say, "Wow, she really took some time developing her baserunning ability." While the ability to run may be instinctive, the ability to circle the bags efficiently, aggressively, and safely is one that can be learned. A good baserunner is not necessarily a player who possesses

Good baserunning puts pressure on the defense and can turn little innings into big ones.

exceptional running speed. There are several additional factors that can complement a runner's performance on the bases. Cutting down on angles, anticipation, intelligence, and instinct are skills that are developed through experience and practice. Good baserunning is not limited to foot speed.

Although players of all running speeds are responsible for learning the fundamentals of baserunning, you must understand your individual abilities, and, in some cases, limitations. If you have below-average foot speed, you should have a conservative approach on the base paths. Trying to steal bases and trying to stretch singles into doubles may be too risky and detrimental to your team's offense. This does not mean that you should be growing roots in the dirt at first base. Watch the trajectory of the pitch. Assume that balls in the dirt will not be fielded cleanly by the catcher. If the pitch gets away from the catcher, be alert, and get down to second base. In fact, a good rule of thumb to follow is

that any time you see the catcher turn her back to you, you should go, regardless of your base-stealing ability. Keep your mind in the game and take advantage of the defense whenever possible, but be smart when making an aggressive decision.

Batting from the left side gives a hitter a tremendous advantage. Left-handed hitters are closer to first base (they don't have to run as far), and their follow-through creates momentum that helps them get to the base quicker.

OUT OF THE BOX

How fast you get down the first-base line is heavily reliant on how quickly you get out of the batter's box. By simply paying attention and by eliminating any unnecessary movements, you can save quite a bit of time. The instant you hit the ball and release the bat, drive your right arm forward as you push off the left leg if you are a right-handed hitter. (Lefties should drive the left arm and push off with the right leg.) Keep your head up, your eyes forward, and your arms pumping. Your first steps out of the box are short and choppy and on the balls of your feet; then lengthen your stride and sprint as fast as you can toward first. Keep your body relaxed and loose to eliminate any tension. Tension has a negative effect on your running speed.

No matter where you hit the ball, run to first base at full speed. Even the very best fielders make errors, so make sure you are hustling to take advantage. A pop fly can be misjudged. A routine ground ball may be bobbled. A slow roller down the line might hit a pebble and bounce fair. Every time you make contact,

We try to identify the kids as turtles or rabbits, so that they know. Too often you get turtles who think they are rabbits.

—Cindy Cohen, head coach, Princeton University

give it everything you have to get down the base line as quickly as possible. Extra-base hits are often made or lost by how quickly you break from the batter's box. Hustling is the best way to play the game.

If you find that your sprint to first is slower than most, try breaking down the sprint to recognize where the problem lies. You may simply have slow foot speed, or possibly there is a problem with your running form. Time yourself for just the first twenty feet out of the box and compare it to the times of other players at that distance. If you are much slower, then your technique getting out of the box is your problem, not speed. Are you holding on to the bat too long? Are you watching where the ball is going? Are you not pushing off your front leg? Are your elbows flying out? Create a checklist to isolate your problems. A common mistake is that runners slow up as they near the first-base bag. Make sure you run through the bag at top speed. Imagine the base is ten feet beyond its actual position.

RUNNING TO FIRST

The shortest distance between two points is a straight line. This fact holds true even on the softball diamond. Run a direct line to first base just outside the foul line. This is called the running lane, and it keeps you safe from any interference call if you are hit by a throw. Find the running lane immediately, and run as fast as you can straight through the base. Do not change your strike to lunge for the base, and don't slide; both techniques will slow you down. Also, do not turn your head to peek at what the in-fielder is doing. It will cost a few fractions of a second, which could be the difference in being called safe or out.

You want to overrun first base by quite a bit (unless the first baseman is going to try to tag you out, which would be the only

TEACHER'S TIP

Patty Gasso, the head coach at the University of Oklahoma, has a surefire way of breaking her players of the bad habit of watching their hits as they run toward first. She videotapes them.

"When the girls swing the bat and connect, it is the first thing you see. They are watching their hit. They do not believe it. But get them on videotape," Patty advises.

"I had a leadoff hitter who was one of the fastest kids in the country. She was stealing fifty-odd bases; second in the nation. She was a left-handed slapper, and I got her on video. She would be running down to first and looking back the whole way to see if the ball is fair or foul. So she was not getting ultimate speed. It didn't usually matter because she could get to first with her speed, but if the ball went through to the outfield, then she may have been able to take second if she maximized her speed.

"And videotape them when they do not know you are doing it. You can tell them again and again, and they think they understand, but when they see it on videotape, they'll see your point."

3

On a ball hit safely to the outfield, bow outward (toward foul territory) as you approach first base. This creates an angle that allows you to run toward second base on a straighter line. Bow out gradually so that you can maintain good running speed.

time you might want to slide). You may turn toward second base if there is an overthrow. The first-base coach should advise you if you should continue on to second base or not. If she tells you to go to second base, do it without hesitation. Trust the advice of your first-base coach because she is watching the play develop for you. That is why she is there. But don't be totally reliant on the coach for direction, either. Any overthrows that travel down near the right-field line will be in your field of vision, thus allowing you to make a quick decision as to whether and how far you can advance.

When you reach first base safely (and there is no overthrow), go directly back to the bag. Do not move toward second unless your first-base coach tells you otherwise. Even if you appear to be moving toward second base, you could be tagged out. Your grand efforts toward making it to first base are suddenly wasted.

TURNING THE CORNER

When luck is on your side, ground balls off your bat find holes in the infield. You have done your job with the bat; now it is time to focus your talents on running the bases. Once you see the ball skip into the outfield, run hard and make an aggressive turn after touching first base. Getting the ball through the infield will get you to first base. Being aggressive out of the batter's box may have you smiling on second.

Aggressive baserunning can cause the defense to make mistakes. It's your job to take advantage of any miscues in the field.

Don't slow down or break stride as your reach first base. Touch the base on the inside corner (closest to the pitcher) and push into a direct line toward second base.

When you crack a ball through the infield and the first-base coach tells you to turn the corner, approach the bag at an angle. About fifteen feet before you get to first base, bow out to your right a bit and then head back in toward the base, making a slight arc, which will allow you to approach second base on a more direct line. The arc should not be too big—about four to six feet is enough—or you will waste more time than you will save. After you flare out a bit, drop your left shoulder in toward the base. This gives you leverage to accelerate through the bag and on toward second base.

Touch the bag on the inside corner with the foot that comes up first as you're sprinting. It's preferable to use your left foot to gain a more direct route to second base. Stepping on the bag with the right foot sends you arcing a bit toward the outfield, but at times the right foot will come up as you approach the bag. Do not stutter-step so the left foot will step on the bag. It takes too much time and slows down your momentum. Do what comes naturally and avoid breaking stride. Stopping and starting near the bag is an easy way to tangle your feet and risk an injury.

Always make a strong turn toward second base. Even on a routine ground-ball single to the outfield, take your turn with the idea that you're headed to second base. Pick up the ball in the outfield to see if the outfielder has fielded the ball cleanly. If she bobbles the ball or if it gets by her, keep it in gear and advance to second base. Always anticipate that the ball will be misplayed, and you won't miss any opportunity to advance.

LEADS

Once you are on base, your goal, as always, is to get to the next base. To increase your chances, take an aggressive lead off the bag. Take every lead like it is a potential steal. By leading off the bag with the same vigor every time, it is much easier to fool the defense when you get the steal sign. Head back to the base quickly if the hitter does not connect with the ball. An alert catcher will whip the ball to the base, picking off any day-dreamers. And never take your eyes off the ball.

The length and style of your lead depend on the base you are on. When leading off of first base, place your left foot over the front right corner of the bag and place your right foot directly behind the bag in foul territory. Crouch low to the ground and face second to put yourself in good position to steal a base or to advance on a wild pitch. If you are only leading, then push off the base, turn your body to face the hitter, and take two or three shuffle steps. A shuffle step is a short hop that moves your body sideways toward the next base as your feet shuffle underneath you.

On second base, you can take a bigger lead. Your goal is to score on a base hit, so get off the base as far as possible. Run three our four steps toward third base and then turn your body to face the hitter and shuffle step. Watch out for a middle infielder who sneaks over to second base after the pitch. A catcher who has a good arm may try to pick you off. On third base, your lead

Lead off first base with the anticipation of a sprinter waiting for the starting gun.

5

should be as far as the third baseman allows you to go. If she's not within a few feet of the bag, there is no reason you should be either. Always anticipate that every pitched ball will be hit or will slip past the catcher. Alert, aggressive baserunning is often the deciding factor in a close game.

Keep track of where the infielders and the outfielders are positioned as well. If the outfield is playing deep, you may be able to take an extra base on a ball hit to the outfield. How shallow or how deep the infielders are playing can also dictate your decisions on the base paths. If you are on third base with fewer than two outs, you and your coach have to decide if you are going to take off for home plate on a ground ball or hold the bag. If the infield is playing at normal depth (in their normal positions), you're running home on a ground ball. If they're playing up (shallow), you will probably hold on a ground ball and make sure it goes through the infield before running.

STEALING SECOND

Stealing second base is a combination of speed, good running form, and getting a good jump. A common misconception is that only the fastest runners can steal bases. Many players with great speed have difficulty stealing bases, whereas other players with average speed, steal bases with ease. A good base stealer makes keen observations, anticipates well, and is alert to the defense.

Most coaches time their players in a sprint to first. Find out what your time is. Does it match your expectations? If you are running a 2.7 or a 2.8 and you are not stealing many bases, you need to be more aggressive. If you are making those attempts but are constantly getting tagged out, you know it is not your speed but your technique. On the flip side, if it takes you four seconds to sprint sixty feet, stealing bases simply may not be in the cards.

When stealing second base, set up exactly the same as with all your other leads. As soon as the pitch is released, push off the bag and go. No shuffle step this time. Break for second base and immediately look at home plate to see what the batter does. If the batter makes contact, a quick glance will tell you what type of hit it is. If it is a pop fly, get back to first base quickly. On a base hit, the runner should look to advance to third base. Find your third-base coach and follow her instructions.

If no contact is made, put your focus back on the bag and continue your torrid pace to the base. As you get to within about ten feet of the bag, break into your slide. (Sliding will be discussed in detail later in this chapter.) Pay attention to where the infielder is taking the throw. This may influence where you slide and what type of slide you decide to use.

Steal second base by pushing off the base with your left leg as the pitcher releases the ball. After a few steps, glance toward home plate to make sure that the ball isn't batted into the air.

RUNNING ON A HIT

How well you run the bases is largely dependent on instinct. Good baserunners always seem to get a good jump and have a nose for knowing when to take the extra base. As we mentioned earlier, softball instinct is built through playing experience and practice. Running base to base, however, relies on what the hitter does with the bat.

Any time you're on first base and the batter hits a ground ball, take off. If you are on second base or third base, the situation dictates when you run. (This will be covered later in this chapter.) If a fly ball is hit, run about halfway to the next base. Do not automatically head back to the base, because if the ball is dropped, you are an easy force-out and lose the chance to advance a base. If the ball is caught, retreat to the bag. Of course, if there are two outs, you are running as soon as the hitter makes contact.

Two unwritten rules in baserunning are never to run into an out, and never to make the first or the third out at third base. The first simply means that if a defensive player is holding the ball, don't run to her and allow her to tag you. Force her to make a throw or at least delay the inevitable by making her come to you. For example, if you're on first base with one out and a ground ball is hit to the second baseman, you are taught to run hard to second base. But if the second baseman fields the ball in your path to the base, do not allow her to tag you out. Stop in your tracks. This

Be an observant baserunner. Know the running ability of other baserunners and where the infielders and outfielders are positioned. Do your homework before the ball is put into play.

forces her to make the throw to second (which could be an errant throw) or run after you to tag you out. Either way, it takes the second basmen more time to get you out, which could eliminate the chance of completing the double play at first base. If you run into the tag, she only needs to flip the ball to first for the double play. If it is a situation where there's no force play, get into a rundown. (Rundowns are discussed in detail later in this chapter.) Rundowns often cause all kinds of problems for the defense.

The second unwritten rule is never to make the first or the third out at third base. If you are safely at second base with no outs, a bunt, ground ball, passed ball, wild pitch, base hit, slap hit, or deep fly ball can advance you to third base. A runner on third base can then score on a routine fly ball to the outfield or even a ground ball to the infield. To make the final out of the inning at third base is also reckless base running. Think about the situation. If you're safe at second base with two outs, it takes at least a base hit to score you. It's the same scenario at third base, so why take the risk of trying to make it to third base?

THE SLIDE

One of the most exciting plays in softball is sliding into a base. It occurs when there is a close play on the bases and you've got to hit the dirt if you hope to be safe. Players often question why slid-

The most common method of sliding is the bent leg slide. Throw your arms up in the air and land on your rear end. Bend one leg underneath you, and stretch out for the base with the opposite leg.

ing is necessary. Well, if you enjoy being on base and want to stay there, sliding will become a part of your game.

Suppose you are running at top speed into second base. To stay on the base and not run past it, you have to slow down as you approach the bag. Putting on your breaks prematurely adds to your running time between bases. Sliding allows you to run into the base at top speed. Secondly, sliding makes it more difficult for the fielder to tag you out. If you go into the bag standing up, the fielder can tag you from your head to toes (a span of four to six feet in height). The incoming throw can be high or low without losing any advantage. If you slide, the fielder is forced to bring her glove to the ground. On a high throw, you can slide safely under her glove.

Many players do not realize that an improper slide can cause injury. You should practice sliding in some soft sand, or wear sliding pads during practice, so you have already perfected the technique before game time. Conversely, you also can injure yourself by not sliding: Stopping yourself from a full sprint while trying to stay on the bag can cause sprains, tears, and twists. Be aggressive in your sliding motion. Good sliders have a knack of lowering their center of gravity as they approach the base, so that their slide is very explosive.

There are a number of different slides to try. Start out with feet-first slides, because they are the easiest and the safest to learn. The most common feet-first slides are the bent-leg slide, the hook slide, and the fake hook slide. You may feel comfortable with

Kids ask, "Do we have to slide in practice?" I answer, "I don't know. Do you have to slide in a game? Yes? Then I think you should slide in practice."

—Cindy Cohen

To use the pop-up slide, slide into the base as you would for a bent leg slide, but reach for the base with your heel of your lead foot instead of the toe. As your heel hits the bag, pop up into a standing position. This is one continuous motion.

one type of slide or you may vary your technique depending on the situation. As you progress and get older, you may want to try the head-first slide. In college softball the majority of slides are head-first.

When you slide feet-first, begin your slide by throwing your hands up in the air. This act alone saves you from many common sliding injuries. Aim to land on your bottom, with your feet going forward and your body leaning backward. Break into your slide at least ten feet from the base. Allowing yourself to get too close to the bag can result in injury.

A bent-leg slide is when one leg is bent under the other. The bent leg takes the weight of the slide while the other leg is stretched outward reaching for the base. The player can then use her bent leg and the firm prop of the base to stand up quickly, which could be helpful should the throw to the base miss its mark. This is referred to as a pop-up slide.

The hook slide is used to avoid a tag. When you notice that the fielder is moving to a specific side of the base to catch the throw, slide to the opposite side of the bag. Then, as you are about to slide by the base, bend the leg closest to the base and hook your toe on it, allowing your other leg to slide by.

A similar slide is the fake hook or the fake grab slide. The fielder expects you to hook your leg on the base, so she will put her glove there to tag you out. Instead, you slide past the base, roll over onto your stomach, and grab the base from behind with your hand.

Finally, there is the head-first slide, essentially a dive, where

you reach the bag with your hands. It is probably the quickest way to go into second base on the steal. Push forward and off the ground, with your legs reaching out with your arms. Keep your head up to avoid scraping your chin or getting a mouthful of dirt. These motions should allow you to land on your upper thigh or pelvic area. You generally want to make your slide to one side of the bag or the other.

Do not slide head-first into home plate! In a battle between

To perform the hook slide, slide to the opposite corner of the bag from where the defensive player is positioned (12). Delay your slide so that all of your body travels beyond the base. Grab the base with your inside arm (13). Reach over to touch the back of the base with your other arm (14).

the catcher's equipment and your face, you lose. If you're trying to avoid a tag at the plate, use a hook slide or a fake hook.

GAME SITUATIONS

Part of being a good base runner is being aware of the game situation. You always need to know the score, the inning, and the number of outs. Alert yourself to who else is on base, where the fielders are positioned, who is at the plate, and who is waiting on deck. For example, if you are on second base with two outs and a weak hitter is up to bat next, it is worth the risk to attempt to score on a base hit to the outfield. Even if the outfielders are playing in close and have excellent throwing arms, it's a good time to take a risk. The alternative is to play it safe and stay on third where you may be stranded by your team's weakest hitter.

Practice your baserunning in gamelike situations to prepare yourself for live action. If your defense is working on situational plays, for instance, jump in there and get into the action. This is how you build instincts on the base paths.

The situations are endless, but here are some of the most common base running challenges:

FIRST AND THIRD

If you are on first base with a teammate on third, you are in a great situation to steal second, especially if you are in high school, where defenses are not quite as skilled. Second base will be an easier theft because the main concern of the defense is the runner on third base. Once the ball is thrown through to second base, the runner on third is instructed to break for home. The defense will then cut the ball off before it gets to second base to try to get the runner going home. This allows you to slide in safely, uncontested.

When you are the runner on third, come off the base slowly. As soon as the ball goes over the pitcher's head to second base, you break. Make sure the second baseman does not step in front of second base to cut off the throw. If you notice her creeping forward in front of the bag, you may want to hold at third base to play it safe. The double steal is one of the most difficult plays to defend against.

FLY BALL TO THE OUTFIELD

When a fly ball is hit with fewer than two outs, you usually end up right where you started. However, that does not mean to stand on the base waiting for the next hitter. If you are on first or second, go about half the distance to the next base just in case the ball is dropped. Make sure you go halfway and not ten feet off the base. Unless you are halfway, you will never be able to advance on an outfielder's miscue.

If you are on third base with fewer than two outs, *always* tag up on fly balls hit to the outfield. Stay on the bag until the ball is in the fielder's glove. The moment it is touched, take off for home. Make sure the ball is hit deep enough so you can score. On balls hit to the shallow part of the outfield, attempting to score may be too risky. If you are uncertain, listen to your third-base coach. Running from third base to home is not a time to gamble, especially in a close game. You may be better off giving the next batter an opportunity to knock you home.

A frequent mistake made by runners at third is running home as soon as the ball is hit because they assume it's going to drop in for a single. If the ball stays in the air longer than expected or if an outfielder makes an outstanding play, the runner has to retreat to third. There is no chance of tagging up at this point. Here is how to avoid making this mistake: Any time the ball is hit in the air (a line drive or a pop fly), go back to the base. If the ball drops in for a hit, you can practically walk home. If it is caught, at least you are in position to tag up. Do not get caught off third base on a fly ball. It could cost your team a run.

Always think ahead when standing on third base. You are only sixty feet from scoring a run, so take advantage of any opportunity to make it to home plate. For example, if the ball is hit into short outfield territory, you normally would not tag up. Pay attention to who is catching the ball. If an infielder makes a catch running away from the infield, take off after the catch. With her momentum going toward the outfield, she will probably not be able to throw you out. If the outfielder is coming in to make the catch and has to leave her feet (dive), you should be able to score easily.

If you are on first when a runner is ready to tag up on third, you might want to take the opportunity to tag up yourself. The fielders are going to be far more concerned with preventing the run, and they will be throwing home, not to second.

BASE HIT TO THE OUTFIELD

When there is a base hit to the outfield and you are a runner on third, you will score easily. However, scoring from second base on a hit is not simple. Pay attention to what the third-base coach is telling you, but always assume you are going to score. Start to make a turn as you approach third base that will give you the best running line to home plate. Run full speed and pay attention to what your third-base coach is telling you. By checking the outfielder's position and knowing her arm strength, you should already have a good idea if your coach is going to send you home. However, if it's too risky to advance, she can stop you before it's too late.

If you are the runner on first base, there are a few factors to take into consideration. On a ball hit to right field, especially deep

BASERUNNER'S TIP

There are a few things you never want to do in a slide:

• Never put your hands or arms on the ground first. You can scrape your palms and elbows, bruise your hands, or sprain your wrist.

• Do not start your slide too late or you will jam your leg on a stationary base. Make sure your slide starts at least ten feet from the bag.

• Do not jump into the slide.

• Do not change your mind about sliding. When in doubt, always go for the slide.

• Do not go into home plate head-first.

Softball rules permit runners to leave their base once the ball is released by the pitcher. Take advantage of this by being in motion when the ball is hit.

right, you can probably take third easily. If it is hit to left, you should probably hold up at second. Have a good idea where all the outfielders are positioned. This will help you make your decision on the bases quickly. If the center fielder is playing deep and your teammate hits a single up the middle, you have got a much better chance of making it to third base safely than if she were playing shallow. Whenever possible, force the outfielders to make an aggressive throw. Applying this sort of pressure forces defensive mistakes.

RUNNER AT SECOND—NO FORCE

Once you are standing on second base, you are halfway home. A ground ball to the infield can move you to third base or strand you at second. Pay attention to where the ball is hit. If there is a ground ball to the right side (second-base side) of the field, go to third. A grounder anywhere else in the infield means you hold up. The only exception would be if the ball is somewhat up the middle and the shortstop is going to have to move to her left. With this type of hit you can generally trust that she will go for the play at first rather than third. Also, make sure the ball gets by the pitcher on balls hit up the middle. If she fields it and turns to you, you're a dead duck.

On a ball that is hit to the left side of the field, you can also take off for third after you see the shortstop or the third baseman

throw the ball to first. By the time the ball travels the distance from third to first and back again, you are safe at third. You must be sure you can advance to third base without risk. Remember, you are already in scoring position on second. Don't kill a rally by becoming adventurous on the base paths.

Always understand the game situation when standing on second base. How aggressive or cautious you are will be largely determined by the score, number of outs, whose on deck, and what inning it is.

ADVANCING ON A SACRIFICE BUNT

A sacrifice bunt is when a hitter sacrifices a swing to bunt the ball and advance a baserunner. If you are that runner, your job is to move to the next base, and because your team is sacrificing an out, you better get there.

If you are on first base when a sacrifice bunt is called, your responsibility is pretty obvious. Get to second. You also may have an opportunity to get to third. Pay attention to what the fielders are doing. Chances are that the corners are moving in, the second baseman is covering first, and the shortstop is trying to stop you at second. Who is covering third? Some teams have the pitcher head to third, but others let her charge the plate for bunt coverage. This is the time to make your move. If the bunt is good and they have to throw to first, think about taking third while they are making that play. Not only is it a long throw across the field, but also the base may be open. See the ball on the ground before you try to advance. Running on a ball that is bunted in the air can result in a double play. Also, if the batter bunts through the pitch (misses it), get back to the base. It offers a catcher an excellent op-

In a rundown, the primary goal of the baserunner is to avoid being tagged out. The secondary goal is stay in the rundown for as long as possible, thereby allowing other runners an opportunity to advance.

portunity to pick you off.

RUNDOWN

A rundown is when you (the baserunner) are caught between bases and an infielder is chasing you with the ball. Her job is either to catch you and tag you out, or to run you to a base, flip the ball to her teammate, and have her tag you out. Your job is to stay alive as long as possible and to get back to a base safely in any way possible.

If you are caught in a rundown, your best hope is for the defense to make a mistake. With this in mind, you want to get the defense to throw the ball as much as possible. Ideally, you also want to try to run to the next base, but your first priority is getting to any base safely. Margie Wright, the head coach at Fresno State, has an unusual trick. She tells her players, "If you are caught in a rundown, and they are running right at you, drop to the ground, roll past them, and go." She's experienced some success with that. Staying in a rundown may also allow the other baserunners to advance.

DRILL TIME

BASE RACE

This is a good drill for teaching your baserunners to cut tight corners and get around the bases as fast as possible. Set up an infield with no pitcher. Your baserunner tosses the ball to herself and hits a ground ball. She then takes off around the bases as fast as she can, going from first to second to third to home. The infield also circles the bases with their throws, trying to get the ball to home plate before the runner gets there. If it is an inexperienced team, it should be about even. More advanced teams have to take the ball back to first each time—that is, field it, go to first, go to second, back to first, go to third, back to first, and then home. The person who fields the ball is not allowed to be involved in covering

a base, just as it is in a game. Every baserunner who makes it home before the ball gets a point. Make it a contest to see who can get the most points.

TEAM SLIDING

Sliding practice can be turned into a fun game. Divide the team into groups of four. One group of four should move out to a square area (about twenty by twenty feet) marked on the field, with a "base" in each corner and a player on each base. At the whistle, the player at home takes off for first, sliding in. When she touches the bag, the player standing there at first takes off for second. When she slides in, the runner on second base takes off toward third. This continues around the horn until the player who began at home gets back home again. Whichever team does this the fastest is the winner. If you do not have enough room to have all your groups going at once, then you can use a stopwatch to see which group is the fastest.

You also do not have to make this a competition. Use the regular infield and divide the team into four groups, putting a group at each base. Start each base at the same time so that four players are running and sliding at once on the same infield.

The outcome of a play at the plate may depend on the efficiency of your turn coming around third base, how well you lead off base, or how much you knew about the positioning and arm-strength of a fielder.

I think one of the best things that we do is base running drills in practice. We make sure there is a defensive play that the fielders are working on also. Once we've gone through the techniques of telling someone how we want them to run the bases, how we want them to take their leads, then we actually make them practice it.

—Ralph Weekly, coach of the national team and head coach at University of Tennessee, Chattanooga

THE DEFENSIVE GAME

THE FUNDAMENTALS OF DEFENSE

A ccording to Ralph Weekly, coach of the national team, "The best defensive skill you can have is focus," and few coaches would disagree. On the field, you have to be completely aware of every aspect of the game. Always keep in mind what inning it is and the score of the game. Know how many outs there are and the speed of the runners on base. Keep track of what the count is on the batter, what type of a batter she is, and where she usually hits the ball. Even if you are the right fielder and she's a left-handed slap hitter, assume the ball is coming to you and think about where you will be throwing the ball when you field it. Do your homework on the field before the pitch is thrown. It might mean the difference between a ball hit just out of your reach and a routine out in the scorebook.

Mental preparation makes your job on the field much easier. Before each pitch, make sure your positioning on the field makes sense. If a right-handed hitter just pulled two fastballs foul, take a couple of steps to your right. Remind yourself where you are going to throw the ball if it is hit to you. If you are mentally prepared, playing good defense is reduced to catching and throwing the softball.

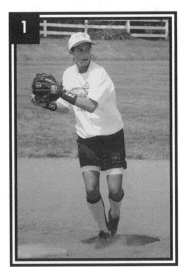

Nothing inspires a pitcher more than having a good defense behind her.

Grip the ball across the laces with the middle three fingers, and place the thumb and pinkie finger along the sides for support. The ball is held in the fingers, not in the palm of the hand (3).

Throwing the ball and catching it are the first skills you learn in your backyard. As simple as both may sound, you need to work on performing each the correct way. With plenty of practice you will begin to build the foundation of a solid defensive player. A great hitter is exciting to watch three or four times every ten at-bats. A great defensive player is reliable ten out of every ten chances.

THE PROPER WAY TO THROW

No one likes to hear, "You throw like a girl!" It has to be one of the most irritating insults in the sport. Nonetheless, you are well aware of what that statement means. For some reason, many girls (and some boys) new to the game tend to push the ball out of their hand, snapping their elbow rather than snapping their wrist. The wrist snap is crucial to proper throwing technique and is very simple to learn.

All positions on the field differ in some way, but you have to be able to throw the ball to play any of them with success. Throwing is very important, and you should work on the fundamentals every day. To start, bring the ball into the cradle position, right

You need to pick a defensive situation every day and put about twenty hard-core minutes into it. There's nothing worse than getting in a game situation and not acting it out.

—Cindy Cohen, head coach, Princeton University

I'm not real big on a lot of special things. I think it's a game of playing catch and being able to throw it and if you can do that, then I think you can defend people.

—Mike Candrea, head coach, University of Arizona

underneath your chest. Pretend you are holding a baby in your arms and you have found the cradle position. Now grab the ball with two or three fingers (depending on the size of your hand) across the seams, using your thumb as a guide on one side and the ring finger (for the two-finger grip) or pinkie (the three-finger grip) on the other. This grip keeps the ball in your fingers and out of your palm. Keeping the ball in the fingers ensures a loose grip, which is what you want. Gripping the ball back in your palm promotes a tight grip, which will decrease the speed and carry of your throw. Place your fingers across the seams to help you get a more secure grip.

Before you throw the ball, take a short step *toward* your target with the foot that is on the same side of the body as your throwing hand. This gets you in position to throw. Some players erroneously take a step backward in an effort to set up. This takes you farther away from the target and tilts your body back, placing all your weight on the back foot.

As you begin your throw, step toward the target with the foot on the glove side of your body. As you step, push (separate) your upper arms outward. From here you go into what Olympic third baseman Lisa Fernandez refers to as the "Arnold Schwarzenegger." Your front arm extends out toward the target, and the back arm is in an upward L. Your shoulders and arms should be in a straight line with the target.

This next step will prevent you from "throwing like a girl." Bring the ball up forward to your ear with your palm down. When

FIELDER'S TIP

You want a glove that suits both your position and your size. Do not assume that the bigger the glove is, the easier it will be for you to catch with it. Choose one that fits well and that does not feel too heavy for your hand to get the ball in and out of the glove quickly. A smaller glove makes the ball more accessible. This is especially important for a middle infielder turning the double play. Adult-size infielders should have a glove that's about 12 inches to 12³⁄₄ inches from the heel of the glove to the top of the fingers. Outfielders can get a slightly bigger glove with a deeper pocket. The glove should be 12 inches to 13 inches.

Once you have chosen your glove, break it in properly. Some players flatten their gloves so they look like a taco and open and close it like a book. Do not follow this method. There should be a U or a horseshoe shape in the heel of the glove when you break it in. This is achieved by bringing the thumb of the glove over to the pinkie, and the pinkie is tucked into the thumb. Sometimes the pinkie finger is not strong enough to move that stiff new glove. In this case, put your ring finger in the pinkie slot as well to get more power there to break it in. You can even put your middle finger in the ring finger slot. This motion will create the U shape for your glove.

To make your glove more flexible, you can soften it up in a number of ways. The most common way is with glove oil, but there are other options. The cheapest and most readily available is boiling water. Put some on the areas you need to soften. Do not dunk the entire glove in water, however. You can also apply a very thin layer of shaving cream as long as it contains lanolin.

your palm is down, you have no choice but to snap your wrist when you follow through. A lot of girls bring the hand up with the wrist cocked and the palm up. This is completely wrong.

As your arm accelerates into the throwing motion, pivot on the ball of your back foot. This allows your hips and legs to add strength to your throw. Your glove arm is going to drop down by your hip. Your weight shifts from the back leg to the front leg as you transfer your weight. Keep your throwing hand level with your head and your palm facing down. Then snap your wrist as you release the ball and follow through. Feel the ball release out of your fingertips, and imagine throwing your fingers through your target. That puts backward rotation on the ball, giving your throw better carry.

Just as with the strength of a hitter's swing, the follow-through is very important. The throwing motion is no different. You must follow through on your throws to get good carry on the ball and maximum velocity. Following the release, your throwing arm crosses your body and comes down on the opposite leg, although you do not actually have to touch the leg. The lower you come down on your opposite leg, the harder the ball is going to be thrown. If you are an outfielder, swing the arm all the way down to ankle level because you have longer throws. As an infielder you have to be quicker, so your follow-through comes right around the top of your knee.

If you are struggling with your throwing motion, isolate the arm movement by getting down on the knee on your throwing side. It will help you concentrate on these mechanics without hav-

Remove the ball from the glove, extending your throwing arm behind you. Next, stride with your front foot and point your lead arm and glove at the target while bringing the ball to a position near your ear so that so that your throwing arm is in a cocked position.

You've got to spend a lot of time on throwing drills. When you are in a 1–0 championship game, you can't afford to throw the ball away.

—Ralph Weekly, coach of the U.S. national team and head coach, University of Tennessee, Chattanooga

Drop your lead arm down and pull your glove toward your chest as you begin to shift your weight forward (5). Accelerate your throwing arm directly toward the target, pivoting on your back foot and transferring your weight forward. Finish with your throwing arm across your body as though you were going to reach down and pick something off the ground (6).

ing to worry about your feet or legs. Throw the ball fifteen or twenty times to get a feel for the proper mechanics. Once you become comfortable with your throwing motion, add the lower half of your body.

RECEIVING A THROW

Playing catch is about as fundamental as it gets. But catching the softball is more than just having the glove in the right place at the right time. It takes preparation and concentration. The proper method is to get your body behind the ball, with the glove held up and open. Hold the glove out in front of your body with the fingers pointing straight up toward the sky. Then, as the ball heads toward you, adjust your glove to the location of the throw. If the ball is coming in low, point the fingers down. If it is coming to your right and you throw right-handed, turn your glove over to the right ninety degrees to make the catch.

Always extend your arms out to meet the ball and catch it in the middle of your body. This puts you in good throwing position when you need to get rid of the ball quickly. Catching the ball out to the side forces you to bring the ball back into the center before you make the throw. If the throw is off-center, shuffle your feet to receive the ball in the middle of your body.

As soon as the ball hits your glove, cover it with your other hand. This is just another assurance that the ball will stay in your glove. It also puts you in position to grab the ball with your throwing hand and send it wherever it needs to go. Any college coach will say, "We are a two-handed fielding team."

Make sure you relax your glove arm as the ball hits the glove. Let it give a little, with the force of the ball pushing your arm backward. This keeps the ball from rebounding off your glove, and it gets your hands moving in the right direction for a smooth transfer into your throw.

Position yourself to catch the ball in the middle of your body. Reach for the ball with the glove held open. Keep your throwing hand next to the glove ready to cover the ball as it's caught.

GROUND BALLS

In the U.S. team's debut game in the 1996 Olympic Games, Dot Richardson got the first hit of the game when she smacked a high chopper bouncing to the infield and beat the throw to first. The short distance between the bases (sixty feet) means that routine infield ground balls must be handled quickly. Fielding grounders is one of the most basic skills a softball player learns, and it is also one of the most important.

Fielding ground balls is instrumental in playing good defense. Players at every position on the field should be efficient when it comes to fielding ground balls. That includes pitchers, infielders, and outfielders. Do not rely on batting practice or gamelike situations to give you enough work. Take ground balls every day in practice. Set aside time each day to hone your skills. One good drill to help you improve is to line up across from another player and take off your glove. Have your partner roll the ball to you. Then field it barehanded and throw it back. Do this for about five minutes; then switch. Without the benefit of the glove, you really concentrate on the mechanics of fielding.

Always use two hands when you field the ball. Not only will you stop the ball from bouncing out of the glove, but also you save time making the throw. Your throwing hand will be on top of the ball, ready to grip the seams.

Remembering to use two hands may often slip your mind, but if you practice it enough, you will not even have to think about it before long. Tie a length of string between your two wrists during practice, allowing them to expand only about ten inches apart.

Concentrate on using proper form during fielding drills. The goal is to make he fielding motion become second nature.

Always scoop the ball with two hands. It is not going to take any more time than it takes to pick it up barehanded, and it allows you to be a little more sure of the grip you are going to get.

—Lisa Fernandez, player, U.S. Olympic team

You can even buy a commercial device that does this for you. In this way you always go after balls with both hands. Another trick is to replace your glove with just a flat pad or even a board that you can strap onto your fielding hand. This forces you to trap the ball against the pad with your other hand rather than relying on the pocket of your glove to catch the ball.

INFIELD GROUND BALLS

Becoming a dependable infielder takes practice and great focus on preparation. Making a fantastic diving play or a spectacular leaping catch is entertaining for fans, but your team needs you to make the routine plays consistently. Learn the basics first, then work on perfecting your skills through repetitious training.

First, you should get into the ready position (also called the athletic position). Just as in batting, the ready position gives you balance and the ability to move quickly. For fielding, however, it means that you are facing the batter bent at the waist, your knees flexed, your feet comfortably apart, and your glove hand held out in front of you. On comparing the stance to hitting, there is a little more bend at the waist, more flex in the knees, and a greater distance between your feet.

Your feet should be square, because if one foot is forward you will be at a disadvantage if the ball is hit to that forward side. Square your feet and keep your weight forward on the balls of your feet. Some players like to take a step as the pitch is being

delivered and then immediately get into the ready position. This
is an excellent way to prepare for action. It ensures that your
weight is forward and your body is ready to move. Don't stay back
in the crouched position. You will fall back on your heels and be in
poor position to play defense.

Your arms are relaxed, with the glove out in front, about six
inches from the ground. This is called preparing your glove for the
ball. Some coaches may advise you to place the glove on the
ground, but you may get into the habit of resting your glove hand.
As a result, your reaction time is negatively affected on line drives and hard-hit ground balls. Keep your glove perched above the
ground so it's prepared for any type of ball hit in any direction.

If the ball is coming in slowly or even at a moderate speed, get
to it quickly. Forward movement is imperative. The softball field
is too short to waste precious time waiting for the ball to come to
you. Get in there and charge it. Aside from saving time, charging
the ball will let you play the ball instead of letting it play you. In
other words, you choose which hop you are going to field it on,
rather than taking your chances as the ball reaches you. When
coaches yell, "Don't let the ball play you!" this is what they mean.
Waiting back on your heels is a sure way to encounter a bad hop.

As you make your move to field the ball, get your entire body
behind it. Square your shoulders to the ball and stay low to the
ground. Don't just bend at the waist; use your knees as well. If
you cannot field the ball cleanly, at least try to block it or knock it
down with your body to keep the ball in front of you. If your body

Take a step forward as the pitch is delivered to keep your weight on the balls of your feet.

As a general rule, the closer your position is to home plate, the closer your glove is to the ground, and the farther apart your feet are in the ready position.

—Dot Richardson, player, U. S. Olympic team

It is a lot easier to go up than go down. You are going to be too vulnerable to a ball getting by you if you have your glove up. We try to keep our hands low and in a relaxed position.

—Ken Erickson, head coach, University of South Florida

Always try to get your body in front of the ball. Spread your feet a little more than shoulder-width apart and bend at the knees and waist. Try to get your back parallel to the ground. Hold your glove open and out in front of you (10). As the ball enters your glove, put your throwing hand over the ball. (11). Stay low, because it's easier to come up on the ball than it is to go down.

is not behind the ball and it takes a bad hop, the ball is on its way to the outfield.

Once your body is in position, reach out for the ball with both hands. Keep your head down, and follow the ball into the glove. Players often look up at the last second to see where the runners are on the base paths. Taking your eyes off the ball before it's secure in your glove results in errors. Watch the ball the entire way in, and field it out in front of you.

When you catch the ball, give a little with your arms to absorb the impact, so the ball does not bounce out of the glove. Put your bare hand over the ball to keep it in the glove immediately and get ready to throw. Always remind yourself: *Field the ball with two hands.*

At times, ground balls are hit in your general direction but not straight at you. In this case, get your feet moving to put your body behind the ball. Avoid the habit of stretching out to the side to field the ball. Hustle to get your feet underneath you and in good fielding position.

On a ball that is hit a good distance away, sprint first, showing your side to the ball. Then slow up and shuffle your feet into position. This is more efficient than trying to sidestep or shuffle over to the ball and finding that you have to sprint at the last second. Run hard first and then get your body under control.

Most players use what is called a crossover step to start their sprint. This allows the player to sprint toward the ball, rather

Use a crossover step to move laterally to the ball. To move left, crossover with your right foot. To move right, crossover with your left foot. Square your shoulders to the ball (13) and extend your glove arm to field the ball in front of you.

than sidestepping or shuffling over. To execute a crossover step, step first with the foot that is on the opposite of the direction in which you are running. In other words, if the ball is coming to your right side, step over your right foot with your left foot. This turns your whole body sideways. Because you sprint for only three or four steps, the natural tendency is to move facing the ball. The crossover step puts you in the proper position. Practice this move over and over so it becomes instinctual.

Whenever possible, get your body square to the ball. Avoid fielding it off to the side whenever possible. Fielding the ball off to the side decreases your chances of keeping the ball in the infield. Use a crossover step to get to the spot, then square your feet and midsection to the ball to make the play.

Some ground balls range too far to get your body in front of them. In this case, you have to backhand the ball. This occurs when the ball is hit to your nonglove side and it's either too far over or hit too sharply to have enough time for you to square your feet and get your body in front of the ball. Use a crossover step to get your body sideways to the ball. Run hard to the spot where you will reach the ball. Your final step is a crossover step, and you field the ball off your glove-side foot, reaching across your body with the glove hand. As you reach, turn your glove over so the fingers are pointed down. Keep the glove open and then close it quickly once the ball enters the pocket.

Use this same approach when balls are hit to your glove-hand side. Cross over with your throwing-side foot to turn your body

A right-handed fielder should field a backhand off of her left foot. Bend at the knees and waist and watch the ball all the way into your glove.

sideways. Sprint to the ball on the balls of your feet. Your final step is with your glove-side foot. Reach out for the ball with your glove, secure it in the pocket, get your feet underneath you, and fire a strike to your target.

Sometimes infielders slow up as they get to a ball and then dive for it. Diving for a ground ball is fun, but it's always a last resort. Avoid diving on the ground if possible. It takes a lot more time to get back to your feet and make a strong throw. It may look spectacular to your friends and family in the bleachers, but getting outs is the main concern. However, if the only way to get to the ball is to dive, then by all means go for it.

TEN KEYS TO FIELDING A GROUND BALL

1. Get into the ready position.
2. Lead with your glove hand.
3. Keep the glove and your body low.
4. Reach out for the ball.
5. Keep your head down, and watch the ball into the glove.
6. Always use two hands.
7. Run forward to meet the ball if it is hit slowly.
8. Get your body behind the ball.
9. Catch the ball first, then locate the baserunners.
10. Know where you're going with the ball before it's hit to you.

OUTFIELD GROUND BALLS

A line drive hit over the infield, a hard ground ball that managed to sneak through a gap, or even an errant throw from an infielder are all going to create ground-ball situations for an outfielder. How she fields these ground balls depends on the type of ball hit and the game situation. With no one on base, you can take your time, making sure the runner stops at first. If a runner is on second, it may be a do-or-die situation, and you had better field the ball and get rid of it as quickly as possible.

There are several methods of fielding a ground ball in the outfield, but the first order of business is to get to the ball as fast as you can. Because of this, your ready position differs slightly from the infielder's. Stand upright with a very slight bend in the knees and waist, and hold your glove out waist-high. When you run to the ball, do not carry your glove out, preparing to field the ball. Treat the glove as part of your body, and sprint as you would in a track race. When you slow down your sprint to get your body under control, get into a fielding position. This applies whether you are running sideways or running forward.

When the ball is traveling at a slow pace with no runners on base, field the ball on one knee to make absolutely sure the ball does not trickle by you. As you approach the ball, slow down and then drop down to the knee on your throwing side. Keep your glove to the ground so the ball can't squirt through your legs. You must field the ball in the center of your body. This method of field-

The most important tip to remember when fielding a ground ball in the outfield is to keep your body in front of the ball. You may field the ball like an infielder, or if necessary, drop to one knee to make certain the ball doesn't get by you.

Some situations demand that you field the ball on the run and release a throw quickly. Follow these three steps: 1. First focus on fielding the ball cleanly. 2. Find your target. 3. Get rid of the ball as quickly as possible. Remember, for every step you take with the ball, the baserunner takes two steps.

We do a lot with the do-or-die. A lot of outfielders often don't pay attention to their footing. The people who field off their throwing-side foot often have to take an additional step to make their throw.

—Teresa Wilson, head coach, University of Washington

ing ground balls must be performed only on slow-rolling balls with no baserunners attempting to advance to the next base.

Timing is also important when dropping to one knee. Avoid setting up too early because the ball may take a bad bounce and change direction. If you wait too long, you will have trouble getting into position. Hustle to the ball, but give yourself enough time to get down and block it. On hard-hit ground balls to the outfield, field the ball like an infielder. You'll have better mobility, especially if the ball takes a strange hop. Your positioning also improves for throwing the ball into the field with runners on base. Dropping to one knee on a ball moving quickly can be risky business.

One other method of fielding a ground ball in the outfield is the do-or-die method. It is the fastest method of fielding the ball and getting back to the infield, but also the riskiest. The time to use this is when the game is on the line and a baserunner is attempting to score or advance into scoring position. Once the ball is hit, sprint to it and scoop the ball up on the run. Execute this on the glove side of your body so you can field the ball easily on the run. If you can time it correctly, step with the glove side foot as you field the ball, because it will save time on your throw. For example, if you are right-handed, step with your left foot as you field the ball, your right foot to stand up and grip the ball, and then again with the left foot as you throw. All of this is performed in a continuous motion. It is an advanced method of fielding, but very efficient when mastered.

FLY BALLS

Run on your toes when chasing a fly ball. Running on your heels makes your head move and tracking the ball becomes very difficult.

Two outs, tie ball game, bottom of the seventh. The batter swings, and it is a long fly ball to right. The fielder turns and sprints back to the fence. She finds the ball, she leaps, and she's got it! Good timing and proper fielding mechanics can make the difference between a loss and extra innings.

When you are catching a fly ball in the outfield, judge where you think the ball is coming down first, and move five feet behind that spot. In that way you will take a few steps forward as you make the catch. This benefits your throw because your momentum will be going in the direction you are throwing. Get a mental image of yourself taking two steps forward, catching, then throwing versus taking two steps backward, catching, and then throwing. You'll possess more power behind your throws when you catch the ball moving forward.

Running down and catching a ball that is over your head is more difficult. It takes hours of practice to perfect. You have to turn your back to the ball and sprint as far as you feel is necessary. You cover more distance turning your back to the ball and running, rather than drifting or coasting backward with the ball. Although your back is facing the ball, turn your head a couple of times to keep a continuous watch on the ball. Once you get to the spot of its descent, run a few feet past it. Turn around to the infield and find the ball. If you judged it correctly, simply take a few steps in and catch the ball with two hands over your throwing shoulder.

Even if your starting point is only a few yards away from where the ball will land, get to that spot as quickly as possible and then wait for the ball. If you drift over, your weight will be headed in the wrong direction, rather than toward your throwing target. Also, you may misjudge that ball. Get to the spot quickly so you will have time to make an adjustment. If you're drifting, the ball may fly over your head.

Keep in mind that it takes a lot of practice to get comfortable judging fly balls, but you must trust yourself and develop confidence to become a quality outfielder. Every time a pitch is thrown, you should hope the ball is hit in your direction.

1. Fly balls hit to right field or to left field often carry toward the foul line. This is true on both sides, because if a player is pulling the ball, it tends to hook, whereas if she is hitting to the opposite field, it tends to slice or to tail toward the foul line.
2. If it is a windy day, know the direction of the wind. It affects how the ball is carrying. Know the direction of the wind before the ball is even hit, and then factor in its influence when judging your path to the ball.
3. Take a moment to judge the ball before you make a move. This instant analysis takes a fraction of a second and can save you time, as opposed to moving first and then realizing you have made a mistake.

Always catch fly balls at about shoulder level on the side of your throwing arm. If you catch the ball on that side, your throwing arm is already in position to throw. The time saved by catching the ball over your throwing shoulder can mean the difference between a runner advancing to score a run or being held at third base. Also, plant your glove-side foot ahead of your throwing foot as you make the catch. This leaves you in perfect throwing position. Always remember: For every step you take to get rid of the ball in the outfield, the runner is gaining two strides.

Catching the ball—whether you're playing the infield or the outfield—is the easy part when a ball is hit in the air. The difficult part is getting yourself in position at the spot where the ball is descending. Taking fly balls in practice is a great platform to work on technique, but the best way to improve is during batting practice. There you can work on judging balls off the bat as they're hit off of a pitcher. So whether it's a simple workout or batting practice before a game, go to your position and go after balls as if it were an actual game. Your performance in the field will improve along with your confidence.

You have to think that every pitch that is thrown will be hit to you. If you don't, you are going to have a tendency to lose concentration and will not be ready when the ball is hit to you.

—John Rittman, head coach, Stanford University

DRILL TIME

"RELAY" RACE

Most people know what a relay race is, but they are not thinking of a softball relay. Divide the players into groups of six. Line them up in a long string. The player at the end starts with the ball and, at the coach's whistle, she throws it to the next player who throws it to the next player right on down the line. When the ball gets to the last person, she then throws it back down the line; the first

team to get the ball back to the start is the winner. This drill emphasizes quick releases and accurate throws.

Use your warmup time prior to practice to work on throwing to a specific target. Pick out a spot on your teammate's body and practice throwing the ball there.

TARGET PRACTICE

When fielders throw the ball, it should reach the other player at chest level. This is a drill to help players pay attention to their throwing accuracy. Players should pair up and stand about twenty feet apart. (This distance can vary depending on the skills of the players involved.) The coach blows the whistle, and each pair throws the ball back and forth between each other, trying to make the throws accurate. For each ball thrown at chest level, the pair gets a point. For a ball thrown anywhere else within reach, they get nothing. A wild throw—one that bounces or gets away—costs them a point. Play to a certain number, such as twenty-five or fifty, again depending on the skill level. The pair reaching it first is the winner. The beauty of this drill is that it forces players to throw quickly while still being accurate.

ROUND THE HORN

Divide the players into four groups, putting each group at a base. Start one ball at home plate. The player throws to first and then follows her throw and gets in the end of the line there. The first baseman throws to second, follows her throw, etc. Introduce a second ball once the players get the hang of it.

LEARNING THE POSITIONS

There are many shortstops who can field the ball as well as Dot Richardson does. Several have a stronger arm than Dot does, and even more are quicker and have better range. But Dot Richardson possesses what coaches like to refer to as the "intangibles." She knows how to play her position better than anyone in the world.

Playing good defense takes more than just catching and throwing the ball. You need to learn to play your position. That means understanding where to position yourself on every pitch, knowing where to throw the ball in every situation, and anticipating the risks taken or mistakes made by the baserunners. Good defensive players rarely ponder these tasks during a game; it becomes instinctual.

Every player is expected to field ground balls and fly balls in their area. But they are also required to throw to the proper base or cutoff person once a ball is fielded, cover a base when necessary, and back up teammates who are receiving throws. All these responsibilities are true for every position, but each has some specific demands.

The most valuable players are those who can play many positions.

FIRST BASE

Besides the pitcher and the catcher, the first baseman sees more action on defense than any other player. During the 1996 Olympic Games, U.S. first baseman Sheila Cornell Douty had

fifty-one putouts at first base. Shortstop Dot Richardson made just twelve putouts. As much as you want the quickest and smoothest-fielding players at the second-base, shortstop, and third-base positions, you've got to have a reliable glovesman at first base. Without a dependable first baseman, the talents of the other infielders cannot be maximized.

An outstanding first baseman. one capable of catching balls that short-hop in the dirt, raises the level of confidence of the other players. Infielders need to concentrate on fielding balls cleanly and making a quick throw. If they are concerned with throwing the ball perfectly to your glove, they may slow down their arm speed or throw the ball with less velocity. This leads to errant throws. A first baseman who can come up with (catch) the tough throws along with the routine ones can be very advantageous to a team's defense.

Because there is so much bunting and slap hitting in fast-pitch softball, the first baseman also needs to be agile. She needs to be able to get to the ball quickly to successfully field a bunt or retreat back to the base immediately if the batter slaps the ball. It takes a great deal off the pitcher's mind if she knows she has a good-fielding first baseman. Then the pitcher can worry about throwing effective pitches instead of fielding her position.

BASIC FIELDING POSITION

To set yourself in the ready position at first base, take a fairly wide stance. Spread your feet out a little more than shoulder-

Because the first baseman is often positioned close to the hitter, where lateral movement is less crucial than fielding hard-hit balls, her feet are set farther apart and the glove is touching the ground in the ready position.

With the exception of pitchers and catchers, we recruit the best athletes we can find and make them into what we want. Last year, in the senior class of six, three of them were shortstops in high school. Not one of them played shortstop for me. So we look for their athletic ability. We want to see what kind of foot speed they have, what kind of range they have, what kind of arm strength they have, reaction time, and then obviously all the offensive stuff. But we really take the kids and make them into what we need.

—Cindy Cohen, head coach, Princeton University

width apart. First basemen frequently play in tight to cover the bunt (about forty feet from home plate), which limits the area they can cover automatically (it limits their range), so broaden your stance to cover more territory. Because you play so close to the batter, you'll have little time to react to a hard-hit ball, so get your glove and body down close to the ground. This somewhat limits your lateral mobility, but your coverage is primarily going to be forward and back, with one step to either side.

With no situational cues, such as a bunter or a known slapper up to bat, stand about five or six feet in front of first base. If the batter hits for power, then you might move back to about two feet in front of the base. You should never be even with the base or behind it.

Position yourself one crossover step away from the foul line. This allows you to cover any ball hit down the base line. To check your distance from the foul line, take a crossover step (right leg over your left leg) and reach out with your glove. The middle of your glove should be right on the foul line. Check this when you are in the ready position. Stay low when you take your step. If you stand up when you cross over, you can reach much farther, but that is not how you will field the ball in the game.

Some first basemen play too close to the foul line and cover area that is in foul territory. This reduces your range on the field. Stand closer to the foul line only if it is late in the game when the score is tied or if there is a one-run differential. The object here is to keep runners out of scoring position (off second base). Any ball hit hard down the line is usually a double. To prevent this from happening, move closer to the foul line to make sure nothing gets by you to that side.

PLAYING FOR A BUNT

With a runner on first base, you must be prepared for a bunt. Move up toward home plate. The closer you get to the batter, the closer you should move toward the foul line (but in small increments). For each step you take forward, move about six inches closer to the foul line. You must still protect the line if the batter elects to swing instead of bunting.

If you have quick reflexes, you can be about a third of the way to the plate. Sheila Cornell Douty of the U.S. Olympic team sets up almost halfway to the plate. If your reflexes are only mediocre, play back farther because you will not be able to react if the ball is hit rather than bunted. The closer you get to the plate, the lower you want to be, and that rule of thumb works for every position on the field.

Pay close attention to the batter's hand when you're set in the ready position. If the batter moves her hands up on the bat and then pulls it in toward her body, she's preparing to bunt the ball. As soon as you see her hands move to the bunt position, creep forward. You do not want to sprint, because she still has time to pull the bat back and slap the ball.

Move forward toward the hitter to defend against the bunt.

Assume that any ball bunted down the first-base line is yours. Do not wait for another fielder to make the play. If it's a good bunt (soft and near the foul line), the play will almost always be to first base. Should the batter bunt the ball hard and it gets to you quickly, you may have a chance at getting a force-out on the lead runner (the runner advancing to second or third base). Listen to your catcher for instructions. She can see the base-   runners and will be shouting which base to throw to.

Always use your glove when fielding a moving ball. Attempting to barehand the ball is too risky. Even if the ball is rolling very slowly, scoop or shovel the ball with two hands. It is the safest way to get an out.

DEFENDING A SLAP HITTER

When a slap hitter is at the plate, play about one-fourth of the way to the plate. If you have slow feet, play closer to the base to make sure you can get back to it. Junior teams will often have the second baseman cover first base on the slap hit, but this tactic opens a huge hole on the right side of the infield and offers little chance of forcing a runner out at second base. At the college level the first baseman almost always has the responsibility of covering first base on a slap hit.

Because you have very little time to get back to the base, watch the hitter's hands for any clue as to her intentions. As soon as you see that she is slapping and not bunting, get back to the base. You may be able to detect that a hitter is slapping by watch-

4

To scoop the ball, align your feet with the base you're throwing to, place your glove in front of the ball, and shovel the ball into the glove with your throwing hand.

ing her feet. Some slappers pivot their back foot toward the pitcher before the pitch is released. This puts their feet in position to run at the pitch. Keep an eye on the batter's hands and feet to help you anticipate the play.

RECEIVING THE THROW

Most first basemen have little trouble catching the softball, but faulty footwork is what can lead to mistakes. When the ball is hit on the ground, turn toward the infield and run to first base immediately. By turning toward the infield you'll have a good idea of who is fielding the ball.

When you get to the base, face the infield and stand slightly in front of the bag. Kick the bag (behind you) with your heels so you know exactly where it is. This is very important. You do not want to end up scrambling with your feet to find the bag as the ball is in flight. Square your shoulders to the infielder who has the ball and hold your glove out in front of you to give a good target.

The direction of the throw will dictate which foot you use to step back on the bag and which foot you stride out to receive the throw. When you step back to the base, place your heel on the edge of the base so the ball of your foot is touching the ground. (Do not put your foot on top of the base. You might get stepped on by the approaching runner.) If the throw is on target (at your glove), step back with your throwing-side foot and stride out with your glove-side foot. If the throw is off target to your left, step back to the left corner of the base with your right foot and stretch out with your left foot. On a throw that is off target to your right, step back to the right corner of the base with your left foot and stretch out with your right foot.

The stride (or stretch) for the throw is important on close plays. Stride out as far as you can without letting your foot leave the base. When you stretch out for the ball, you reduce the distance of the throw. Catching the ball a few feet in front of the base can make the difference between the runner being safe or out.

Although your goal is to remain on the base to record an out, *catching the ball* is your first concern. If the throw is significantly off target and requires you to step off the base to catch it, do it. The runner will be safe, but that is better than permitting an overthrow, which may allow the runner to advance into scoring

position. On errant throws to your left, you may be able to leave the bag, catch the ball, and tag the passing runner. Remember, the number one rule for the first baseman is to catch the ball first; worry about the runner second.

Balls that are hit into the outfield gaps are generally considered "sure doubles." This means that the batter will round first base, head for second, and possibly even try for a triple. In this situation you should follow the runner to second base. The middle infielders are headed toward the outfield as cutoff players. On a hit, for example, to the left-center-field gap, the shortstop goes out to be the cutoff, while the second baseman is the backup to the cutoff. This leaves second base open. The first baseman should run to second base in the event of a rundown, or to receive a pick-off throw if the batter makes too wide a turn around second base. Cutoffs and relays are covered in detail in Chapter 7.

To receive a throw at first base, stand with both heels in front of the base, stride to the ball, and catch it out in front of the base.

I love the bad throws. If everyone's throwing it to me right here, right on target, I start to get upset. Come on. Throw it somewhere else, make it a little more exciting.

—Sheila Cornell Douty, player, U.S. Olympic team

THIRD BASE

The third-base position is also known as the hot corner. Batted balls get to you so quickly that you have very little time to react. Any ball hit to you will be either sharply pulled off the bat of a right-handed hitter or a hard slice off the bat of a left-handed hitter. Even slap hitters and bunters keep you busy at third base. Third basemen need to be alert, aggressive, and fearless. There is no time for hesitation down at the hot corner.

I like to have a quick-footed third base-man, so she can cover more territory. The more territory she can cover to the line, the more she can play off the line and in the hole. The more they're in the hole, the more they can allow the shortstop to move over and get the balls up the middle. So if you have a third baseman who can cover some territory, both front and back and right and left, it is advantageous for the whole team.

—Rhonda Revelle, head coach, University of Nebraska

At third base the ready position is similar to that of the first baseman. Stand with your feet spread apart a bit wider than the width of your shoulders. Keep your body and glove low to the ground by flexing your knees and bending at the waist. It is important to stay low since you have such little time to react to the ball. Hold your hands out in front of you, with the glove held open. Keep you eyes focused on the batter.

Stand about five feet in front of the base and far enough away from the foul line so that one crossover step will allow you to touch the line with your outstretched glove hand. Then adjust your position based on the game situation and the skills of the hitter. Is she right-handed or left-handed? Does she bunt frequently? Is your pitcher throwing a lot of off-speed pitches to right-handed batters, causing them to pull the ball? When a power hitter is up with two outs, for example, she is not going to bunt. Move to about three feet in front of the bag. If a slap hitter or a bunter is up at bat, move up to about fifteen feet in front of the bag. Remember: As you move closer toward home plate, move closer to the foul line. As you move back, you can move away from the line to increase your range. Your range is the amount of territory you are able to cover.

If you are playing at an advanced level, watch the catcher set up for pitch location. When the catcher sets up on the outside corner with a right-handed hitter at the plate, the hit will more likely go to the right side of the field; move a step or two to your left. If the target is inside, get ready because the ball may be com-

The third baseman adopts a fielding position similar to the first baseman (feet set more than shoulder-width apart, glove near the ground, in the ready position).

ing your way. Make certain, however, that you are alert on every pitch no matter where the catcher sets her target. The pitcher may miss her spot (location).

Finally, know the fielding skills of your neighboring teammates. Have an idea of how much ground your shortstop can cover. It may allow you to play closer to the line, or force you to move closer to second base. If you have a good-fielding pitcher, it allows you to play deeper and increase your range. If she is slow getting off the mound, you have to play in closer and cover more territory on bunts.

FIELDING THE BALL

The ball gets to you very quickly at third base, so you must be alert and aggressive. Take a step forward as the pitch is delivered. That will keep your weight forward and on the balls of your feet. You may have heard your coach say to you, "Don't let the ball play you." What they mean is to field the ball aggressively with forward momentum instead of waiting for the ball to get to you and fielding it with your weight back on your heels. *Go to the ball.* The longer you wait, the greater chance the ball will take a bad hop, and for every second you wait, the runner takes two to three strides toward first base.

Keep your glove low to the ground as the pitch is delivered. It is much easier to come up for the ball with the glove than it is to go down. Because the distance between your position and the hit-

Since she plays so close to the batter, the ball gets to the third baseman in a hurry. They don't call it the "hot corner" for nothing. This allows you extra time to make a sure-handed grab and a sure throw to first.

I play my position based on the strength of the pitcher. If I have a slower pitcher that people are going to pull, I get closer to the line. If I'm playing with Christa Williams and she is throwing seventy-one miles per hour, then what am I going to do? I'm coming off the line. I yell, "Hey Dot, move over!"

— Lisa Fernandez, player, U. S. Olympic team

On a bunt play, listen to where the catcher tells you to throw the ball. She is facing the in-field and has a clear view of everything that's happening.

ter is short, there is not much time to move laterally (from side to side). For the most part, all you can do is shuffle to either side to get your body in front of the ball.

One advantage of the ball getting to you so quickly is that you'll have more time to make the throw to first base. You do not have to field the ball cleanly every time to get the batter out (although this should be your goal). If the ball is hit to your side or takes a difficult bounce right in front of you, make sure you block it with your body and keep it in front of you. Chances are you will have time to make the play at first base. You may even want to take the mentality of a goalkeeper. Draw an imaginary line perpendicular to your feet and convince yourself that nothing is going to get past that line. And just like a hockey goalkeeper, a third baseman must be fearless.

Although it is referred to as the hot corner, you will get your fair share of weak hits (slow rollers) at third base as well. Between bunted balls and mishits, you need to work on charging the ball and fielding it on the run. Get to the ball as quickly as possible, and scoop or shovel it up with your glove. Do not bare-hand the ball. Set your feet underneath you once you field the ball and find your target, keeping your body in a crouched position. Standing straight up wastes time. Take a step with your glove-side foot and fire the ball to first base. A good drill to practice fielding the bunt is to line up three or four balls about ten feet apart down the third-base line. Then move forward, scoop them up one at a time, and make the throw to first. Do it again throwing to second.

Straddle the bag when await-ing a throw. This puts you in the best position to apply a tag and keeps your legs out of the path of the runner.

    An infielder playing at an advanced level may try to field the ball and throw it on the run (all in one motion). This is very diffi-cult to execute and should not be attempted in a game until it is perfected in practice. The key is to field the ball out in front of you off your glove-side foot. Use two hands so you don't waste time transferring the ball from your glove to your throwing hand. Take one step with your throwing-side foot, then step and throw off of your glove-side foot. This is a tough play because you are still moving forward and the weight of your body is not going toward the target. It takes time to develop the timing, strength, and accu-racy to make this throw. Perfect it in practice, not in the game.

MAKING THE TAG

Every runner attempting to reach third base cannot be a forced-out. She may be trying to steal, coming from second with no one behind her, or trying to stretch a double into a triple. In these cases, the third baseman has to make a tag.

    The ideal position to make a tag is straddling the base. Straddling the base simply means standing with both feet on the ground, with the base between them. When taking the throw at third base, place your right foot on the home-plate side of the bag and your left foot on the left-field side. *After* you catch the ball, bring the glove directly to the ground in front of the base, then react to where the runner's foot or hand is. If you have time (the runner is very late getting to the base) use both hands to make

Tag the runner on whatever part of her body arrives first. If she slides feet first, tag the feet, hands first, tag the hands. The best tag is applied with the ball held securely in the glove by your throwing hand.

the tag. Hold the ball deep in the pocket and either put your throwing hand on top of the ball, or close the glove around the ball and put your hand over the opening. Both methods are acceptable. On a close play (the runner is sliding into the base as you receive the ball), simply sweep the ground with the glove in front of the bag.

Watch the baserunner slide into your glove, just as you watch the pitch all the way in as a hitter. You may have to adjust the position of your glove depending on how and where the runner slides. For example, if the runner slides feet first and is reaching for the left side of the bag with her left foot, tag her left foot. A mistake infielders make is that they simply put the glove down in front of the bag. Good baserunners will slide to a corner of the base to avoid the tag.

Unfortunately, every throw is not going to be perfect. If the throw is off line, move off the bag to catch the ball to make sure it doesn't get past you. Allowing a throw to get past you at third base means a run for the opposition.

THE CUTOFF

On hits to left field with a runner on second base, the third baseman now becomes the cutoff. The cutoff's job is to intercept the outfielder's throw to home plate and relay the ball to the catcher or to another base. There are two reasons for having a cutoff. The first is that most outfielders do not have an arm strong enough to throw a runner out at home plate. A crisp throw to the cutoff, followed by another crisp throw from the cutoff to the catcher, has a better chance of beating the runner than does one long, looping throw from the outfield. The second reason for the cutoff is that if the throw from the outfielder is off line or late, the cutoff can catch (stop) the ball to make sure that no other runners advance.

Once you see the ball get through the infield, position yourself about one-third of the distance between third base and home plate and face the outfielder. As she fields the ball, position yourself so you are in a direct line between the catcher and the outfielder. The catcher will usually help you line up by shouting out, "Two steps to the right" or "One step to the left." Hold both arms up in the air so the outfielder can easily see her target. Set up to catch the ball on the left side of your body. As you receive the throw, open your body toward home plate by stepping in the direction of the catcher with your left foot. Catch the ball, take one step, and immediately throw to the plate. Do not waste time by taking extra steps.

If the ball is off line or late, listen for instructions from your catcher. She may shout, "Cut hold!" This means you should catch the ball and hold on to it. At times the batter may attempt to advance to second base on the outfielder's throw. The catcher may yell, "Cut second!" In this case fire the ball immediately to second base to throw out the runner attempting to advance.

Adjust the position of where you set up for cutoff depending on where the outfielder fields the ball. If she is playing deeper than usual (or has to go to the right or to the left to make the play), move out a little farther. If she fields the ball in the shallow outfield grass, set up deeper toward home plate.

Many amateur coaches instruct their first baseman to take all cutoff throws. If this is the case, simply stay by the third-base bag on hits to the outfield.

MIDDLE INFIELD

The middle infielders are the shortstop and the second baseman. Usually they are the most agile players on the team, since they have to cover a wide range of territory and occupy several roles on the field. Middle infielders are expected to field their position, turn double plays, cover second base on steals, cover bases on bunts, become cutoffs on extra-base hits to the outfield, and back up bases. There is almost always something for a middle infielder to be doing on every play.

Nothing is more important for these middle infielders than having quick feet. If you are a shortstop or a second baseman, make sure you're on the balls of your feet in the ready position. When the ball is hit, you have to be able to move quickly either way. Your feet should be about shoulder-width apart (closer together than for the corner positions), allowing you to move back,

I think the footwork for the middle infielder is one of the most critical things, whether you are fielding a ball or setting to throw or receiving a throw at the base.

— Rhonda Revelle

Middle infielders—the shortstop and second baseman—
are positioned farthest from
home plate and have more
time to get into fielding position. They also have more area
to cover. Spread your legs
about shoulder-width apart
and get set in the ready position.

forward, or laterally in either direction.

POSITIONING

Although the positioning of the middle infielders depends greatly
on the batter's capabilities and the presence and position of runners, it is possible to generalize somewhat. The shortstop and the
second baseman want to play about twenty feet away from second
base and about four to six feet behind the base path. If the ball is
hit to the left side of the field, the shortstop is involved in fielding
the ball while the second baseman covers the bag, and vice versa
if the ball goes to the right.

Game situations often dictate exactly where you get into the
ready position at shortstop and second base. In a double-play situation (a force play at second base with fewer than two outs), play
even with the base path and take two or three steps closer to second base. In a bunt situation, the second baseman has to move
closer to first base if the first baseman is charging in to field the
bunt. When a slap hitter steps up to the plate, the shortstop
should play in closer to get to the ball quicker. Your position in
the middle infield constantly changes, so keep your mind in the
game.

THE UNDERHAND TOSS

When making a force play at second base, the shortstop and the second baseman are usually too close to one another to rear back and make a strong throw. Any time second base is within fifteen feet of where you field the ball, the most common throw is the underhand toss. Throwing the ball underhand gives the player receiving the throw more of an opportunity to see the ball.

After you field the ball, turn your body toward second base. Step toward your target with your glove-side foot and bend your front leg to lower your body. This improves your accuracy. Toss the ball crisply underhand, aiming for your teammate's chest. Your throw should travel on a straight line. If there is any arc to your throw, you're either throwing the ball too softly or are too far away from the base to be throwing underhand. In some situations the force-out at second is the start of a double play, so get rid of the ball quickly.

Stay low to the ground and stride to directly at your target when executing an underhand toss. The ball should never reach an elevation higher than your teammate's chest.

THE SIDEARM THROW

The sidearm throw is for slightly longer throws. The mechanics are similar to a regular overhand throw, but instead of bringing the hand up by the ear, it stays just above the waist. The sidearm throw is efficient for you as a middle infielder because it allows you to release the ball quickly.

Whether you're making a sidearm toss from shortstop (14) or second base (15), get the ball out of your glove early so your teammate can see what angle it's coming from.

To start the throw, the palm faces down as your hand breaks from the glove. Taking your normal step toward your target, turn your wrist and forearm sideways as the arm cocks back to throw. Your arm should be almost parallel to the ground. As your arm moves forward into the throwing motion, it stays along the same plane (almost parallel to the ground). Then the wrist snaps as you release.

The sidearm throw is good for throws that are about fifteen to thirty feet from the bag. Some shortstops use it to throw the ball to first, but a sidearm throw should not be used for throwing across the field. It decreases velocity and accuracy on longer throws, and you can end up hurting your arm. The second baseman can use it on ground balls that move her toward first base, but other than that, its primary use is for throws to second base.

Advanced players execute this throw without taking any steps. They simply field the ball, shift their weight back as they take the ball out of the glove, and shift their weight forward on the throw. Developing rhythm is key to throwing with no step. If you can perform it with strength and accuracy, it saves time.

RECEIVING THE THROW AT SECOND BASE

When receiving the throw on a force-out, it is important to make sure you get the first out before attempting a play on another runner. Make sure you catch the ball with two hands, with one foot on the bag. Some coaches like to tell their middle infielders to become like a first baseman when taking the throw at second

Get the sure out at second base. Use two hands to catch the ball out in front of you, making sure that your foot has good contact with the base.

base. Assuming there are two outs in the inning (the double play is not in order), get to the base as quickly as possible. In that way you will not be moving to the throw, and your teammate will have a stable target. Just as the first baseman does, find the bag first, square your body to the fielder making the play, and then stand just in front of the base. Extend your glove to give a good target. Wait to see the throw before you commit to the ball. If the throw is to your right, put your left heel on the right corner of the bag and stride out with your right foot. If it's to your left, hold the bag with your right heel and stride out with the left.

There will be times when you're running to the bag as the throw is being made. The fielder's job is to throw to the bag rather than to you. Nonetheless, extend your glove out to give her a target. This also prepares your hands for the throw as you're moving. Hopefully, your glove and the ball will arrive at the base simultaneously.

MAKING THE TAG

Proper footwork is important when applying tags at second base. Most throws to second base (when there is no force) come from the outfield. Because each outfield throw comes from a different angle, there is not one specific way to plant your feet at the base. When receiving a throw from the right fielder, square your shoulders to her and straddle the bag with your feet. Point your left foot at the outfielder. Catch the ball and sweep the glove (from left to right) in front of the base. If the throw is off line, leave the base (if necessary) to block the ball.

Take the same stance on throws from center field, though your body will be turned more toward center field. On balls that are hit to the left of center field (left-center or left field), point your right foot at the left fielder while your left foot rests on top of the bag. As you receive the throw, step to the right-center-field side of the base with your left foot and bring the glove down across your body (from right to left) to apply the tag. Adjust your glove position if the runner attempts to avoid the tag.

TAKING THE BALL FOR THE STEAL

Both the second baseman and the shortstop should practice taking throws from the catcher on stolen-base attempts. Most teams have their shortstop cover the bag, but certain game situations may require the second baseman to cover. Straddle the bag, with your left foot on the outfield side of the base and your right foot set up on the home-plate side. After you receive the throw from the catcher, sweep your glove across the base path.

The only time that a second baseman might take the throw is when a slap hitter is at bat. Generally, a slapper attempts to hit to the hole between shortstop and third base. This forces the shortstop to move up and to her right. The second baseman is positioned closer to second base, so it makes sense for her to take the throw from the catcher. When the second baseman covers the steal, she moves to the back corner of the base first, rather than coming across the base line, then straddles the bag to take the throw. Both the second baseman and the shortstop need to be very clear about when they are trading responsibilities for the steal, because if they are both moving to cover, the gaps will be enormous.

THE DOUBLE PLAY

The double play is the pitcher's best friend and goal of the second-base/shortstop combination, and depending on where the ball is hit, there are a number of ways to execute it. If you're a middle infielder and field the ball right next to the bag, take it to the base yourself and then throw to first. If the ball is fielded farther away from the bag, the fielding player feeds it to the covering player who is running toward the bag. No matter how it is done, it must be done quickly. It is also important for the covering player to get out of the way of the baserunner after throwing to first. The baserunner's job is to slide into the player turning the double play. This is called "breaking up" the double play.

If you are a second baseman covering the bag on a double play, you have three options.

1. If the ball is hit hard to third base, you have plenty of time. Straddle the bag and face third base. Step across with your right foot to receive the ball. Catch the ball and plant your weight on your right foot at the same time.

Before the game starts or before an inning, I like to draw myself this little line that goes from the inside corner of the base toward the plate. Now every time I'm going to second base, I'm seeing that line and I'm thinking that there is my position to take the throw from the catcher.

—Jennifer McFalls, player, U.S. national team

There aren't a lot of double plays in softball, but when there is a double play, quite frequently it is because of the efficiency of the footwork of the middle infielder.

—Rhonda Revelle

Drag your left foot across the bag, turn your body to first base, and make an accurate throw to the first baseman.

❷ If the shortstop has to move to her right to field the ground ball, the play must be quick. Step to the inside of the bag with your left foot, catch the throw from the shortstop, drag your right foot across the bag, plant the foot, and throw to first.

❸ If the ball is hit up the middle or to the left of the shortstop, she will deliver the ball with an underhand toss. Place the ball of your left foot on the back side of the bag. After you receive the toss, push your left foot off the base and throw to first base.

If you are the shortstop, you also have three options.

❶ If you have a lot of time, straddle the bag. Receive the throw, drag your right foot across the base, and throw to first.

❷ If the second baseman fields it up the middle, sweep the back corner of the base with your right foot, come across the base, and throw to first base.

❸ Finally, if you receive a throw that takes you to the infield side of second base (most likely from the first baseman), step on the base with your left foot, then step and throw to first.

Here, the second baseman uses classic technique to perform the double play pivot. She steps on the bag with her left foot to receive the throw. After catching the ball, she steps across the bag with her right foot, plants it, and turns to throw to first base.

It is not unusual for a team at an advanced level of play to know what a hitter is going to do at the plate. The scouting has been done. You know whether she pulls the ball, sprays it all over, or goes to the opposite field. You know if she usually tries to go for the long ball or if she is likely to slap or to bunt. You make the adjustments in your position accordingly.

On top of that, you can tweak those adjustments by knowing what kind of pitcher you have on the mound for your team. A really fast pitcher is going to have people swinging late, with not so many pulls. A junkball pitcher might treat you to a lot of ground balls. Take that knowledge and add it to what you know about a batter.

You can also take it one step farther. The shortstop and the second baseman have a pretty good view of the signals the catcher is sending to the pitcher. If you learn those signals, you can use that information as well. For instance, you might have a fastball pitcher on the mound, but she is going to mix it up with some other pitches on occasion. In that case, if the hitter does connect, she probably will not hit it to the opposite field, especially if she is already speeding up her swing to account for the pitcher's fastball. Shift a little before the pitch to take that into account as well. You should also be subtly communicating the signals to the other infielders and the outfielders so that they can make the appropriate shifts, too.

Once the shortstop picks up the sign from the catcher, it's her responsibility to relay the sign to the center fielder.

A rule to remember: A double play means two outs, but you can only get one out at a time. Don't rush. It is better to get the sure out at second base rather than rushing a throw to first base that results in an error. If the fielder bobbles the ball, if you have a poor grip on the ball, or if the runner sweeps your legs out, hold on to the ball. If you throw the ball wildly, the batter may end up on second base.

CATCHER

The catcher, without a doubt, is the leader of the team. Her role is much like a general's. The pitcher and the fielders are her troops. She gives the orders and instructions. The catcher is the final soldier guarding the home base from the opposition. A good catcher is tough, vocal, and intelligent. Solid defensive skills are the roots of a good catcher, but a great catcher possesses defensive skills and strong leadership qualities.

Catching is much more than blocking balls and throwing out baserunners. You need to have a tough personality and a calming presence on the field. You can't be afraid to get dirty and suffer a few bruises behind the plate, and you can't panic when things aren't going well for your team. Pitchers and position players look to their catcher for guidance and confidence.

Catchers should also have more softball smarts than anyone else on the field. You should have the ability to call the pitcher's pitches, and to call plays once the ball is hit. On certain plays in the infield, especially bunts, it's the catcher's responsibility to yell out where the ball should be thrown. You are the only player facing the entire infield, so your teammates need to trust your eyes and judgment. Shout number "One! One! One!" for first base and "Three! Three! Three!" for third base. You must call the base firmly and without hesitation.

> *I do not think you can have a good team without a good catcher.*
>
> *—Cindy Cohen*

THE CATCHER'S EQUIPMENT

A catcher's equipment includes shin guards, a chest protector, a mask, and a glove. Look for a glove you can handle. If it is too heavy, you will not be able to move it quickly enough to stab (block) errant pitches. Your shin guards should fit you perfectly. Do not settle for what your team has lying around if it does not fit. It may hinder your mobility behind the plate.

Most importantly, you need a chest protector and a mask to protect your upper body and face. A catcher should never catch without a mask. It is a safety issue, but it also makes good practice sense. You have to catch with a mask on in the game, so get comfortable doing it all the time. In fact, always practice wearing all the equipment, because you are required to wear it in the game.

> *You have to be a leader. You have to be vocal. That's an important part of the job. You have to be able to direct your team and not be worried about being shy. It is hard for a lot of young kids. Talking is often the hardest thing for them.*
>
> *—Shelly Stokes, player, U.S. Olympic team*

TEACHER'S TIP

When I first started coaching and I was an assistant at Trenton State, we had a pitcher who could flat out throw the ball hard. It was her first year pitching, and you just never knew where that ball was going to go. But we wanted her to keep throwing hard because speed is what you teach first. But she hit the kids. They didn't want to take batting practice. I'd have to say, "She's going to take you to the promised land, you get in here and hit."

We had two catchers. We had a freshman catcher who was a stud, and we had a senior who had really lost some confidence at that time. So this pitcher would throw the ball and it would go flying. And I mean a lot. And this senior catcher would roll her eyes and throw her mask down and generally act disgusted as she went to retrieve the ball. And I can assure you that this did not make my freshman pitcher, who had never thrown in college, want to pitch. Then I had this freshman catcher who had the sweetest temperament in the world. We kept saying she was a puppy that we knew was going to grow up to be a German shepherd. So the pitcher would throw, and the ball would go wild, and the freshman catcher would get up and say, "My fault! I'm sorry! My fault!" That pitcher, who normally was really smart, by the way, started to feel better, and she got confidence, believing that her wild pitches were the catcher's fault. And that pitcher went on to be All-American, and she did take that team to the promised land. So the moral of the story is that your catchers' temperament is important, and so is their ego. Basically, they have to have none. The pitcher's going to have enough ego for everybody.

—Cindy Cohen

THE READY POSITION

Just as you should always practice with your mask on, always practice catching from the ready position. Many players warm up their pitchers by kneeling and sitting back on their heels. Do not make this mistake. Practice catching as if it were a game situation. The only way to develop skills and proper technique behind the plate is to spend every possible moment in the ready position. It's tough activity on your legs, and your calf muscles may ache, but there is no better way to get them in shape for a game.

In the ready position, squat down so your rear end is as close to the ground as possible. Hold your arms and elbows on the outside of your knees. The pitcher's targets are from knee to knee and from shoulder to shoulder. Make sure you are low enough so these points are all in the strike zone. Tuck your throwing hand behind your ankle or keep it behind the glove.

If there is a runner on base, lift up your rear end. Your shoulders stay in the same position, but your back becomes more perpendicular to the ground. Now you are closer to being upright, which allows you to get rid of the ball quickly if the runner steals.

When you are behind the plate, position yourself as close to the batter as you can without getting hit with her swing. This should be about an arm's length away. The closer you are to the plate, the fewer balls will bounce in the dirt and the less distance the pitch will have to travel to reach the strike zone.

With the bases empty, squat in the set position and display a big target for the pitcher (20). With a runner on base, get up on the balls of your feet (moving the left foot slightly in front of the right), lift your rear end, and be prepared to throw the ball or field a bunt (21).

BLOCKING

The ability to block pitches in the dirt is a vital skill for catchers. It saves runs, restrains runners from advancing, and allows the pitcher to pitch with confidence. *Do not* attempt to *catch* pitches in the dirt. This mistake often leads to wild pitches and/or passed balls. Nothing hurts a team more than a run that scores as a result of a passed ball.

There are two ways to block a bad pitch, and they depend on where the pitch is. If the ball is coming straight at you but low, kick your legs back so your knees will land where your toes were. This lowers your body so you can surround the ball with your shoulders and midsection. Do not fall forward onto your knees because your upper body will still be too high. Your glove should be on the ground blocking the hole between your knees.

To block the ball coming to the side, shoot your leg out diagonally toward first or third (depending on the location of the pitch) and parallel to the foul line. This movement allows you to keep your shoulders over the plate. Bring your opposite knee down in the direction of the pitch, and keep both your rear end and your chin down. Again, your glove should be on the ground, covering the hole between your legs.

For both types of balls, tuck your shoulders inward. Stay low and square to the ball. Make sure your weight is forward and your upper body surrounds the ball, which stops it from deflecting far from your body.

Block pitches in the dirt, don't try to catch them. Drop to your knees, fan your legs out to the side, place your glove on the ground between your legs, and try to keep the ball in front of you.

Practice blocking every day so you develop muscle memory. As soon as your eyes see a pitch that is going to be in the dirt, your body automatically goes down to block it. When you practice, have your teammate or coach throw the ball underhand (like a pitcher). Balls thrown overhand bounce a different way and will not be as effective in training you. Wear all your equipment whenever participating in any of these drills, because it's safer and you will be wearing equipment in a game.

FRAMING THE PITCH

Because calling balls and strikes is fairly subjective, the catcher can help the pitcher by the way she catches the pitch. Framing the pitch means receiving a pitch that is on the border or just out of the strike zone and then turning your glove in toward the strike zone as you catch it. The goal is to influence the umpire to call a pitch a strike that he or she may have called a ball. For example, if the pitch is a little high, catch the ball and roll your glove downward. This presentation will give a much better chance of having the pitch called a strike. Many young catchers shoot their glove upward to catch a high pitch, giving the umpire the illusion that the pitch was higher than it actually was. Framing the pitch may help your pitcher get a few extra strikes in a game.

If you are playing at a higher level, where pitchers have excellent control of their pitches, line up your glove and body where you expect the pitch to be. This makes every pitch look like a strike. For example, if you are expecting an inside pitch, put the

23

glove just off the inside corner of the plate and shift your body behind the glove. By catching the ball in the center of your body, the
umpire can be coaxed into believing the pitch is a strike. Do not
make your movements behind the plate obvious. If the hitter
hears you move inside or outside, she can look for a pitch in that
location. Adjust your position when the pitcher begins her
windup.

FIELDING BUNTS

A mobile catcher not only helps the defense when the ball is
bunted, she also helps when the hitter swings away. If the catcher
is quick out of the box, it allows the first baseman and the third
baseman to play a little deeper at their positions. As a result, both
infielders have better range.

The first thing you do when the ball is bunted is take your
mask off. Take it off, throw it out of the way, and find the ball. If
you are comfortable fielding the ball with your mask on, go for it;
it may save you valuable time.

Come out of your squat to field the bunt, but do not come out
of your crouch entirely. By standing up straight, you'll waste precious time. Think about moving forward to field the bunt instead
of standing up and then moving forward.

When you field the ball, get your feet and shoulders in line
with where the ball is going to be thrown. Because you want to
field the ball off your throwing foot, you have to listen carefully to
the shortstop (she will be calling this play instead of you because

*Framing a pitch is a technique
used by catchers to make bor-
derline pitches appear to be
strikes. Wherever you catch
the ball, turn the glove in toward home plate. This pitch
appears as if it might be a little
outside to a left-handed hitter.
But by turning the glove inward, you give the umpire the
impression that the pitch is a
strike.*

*I normally take my mask off when I'm
trying to field in front of the plate, but
there are times when you do not have the
opportunity to do that. Really it is a personal preference with catchers.*

— Shelly Stokes

On foul pops behind home plate, turn your back toward the infield (the ball will spin back toward fair territory), find the ball and get under it, then toss your mask away so that you don't trip on it.

You have to know the other team's strengths. If you play Arizona, and they get a runner on second, you had better know that they are going to try to steal third on you. And if you aren't prepared for that, they'll succeed.

—Ralph Weekly, coach of the national team and head coach, University of Tennessee, Chattanooga

you are the one fielding the ball) before you take that last step. If you do not hear anything, line up for first and get the sure out.

FIELDING FOUL POPS

When a player hits a foul ball high in the air around home plate, the first thing you should do is take off your mask and find the ball. Do not drop your mask. You need to hold on to it until you know the direction in which you are running; then toss it in the opposite direction. If you throw your mask without finding the ball first, you may end up tripping over your mask as you move to field the ball. Foul pops are hit with backspin, so the rotation on the ball makes it carry toward the infield. Factor this in when judging the ball. Since it floats in that direction, it is easier to turn your back to the infield. In this way the ball will come back to you instead of moving away from you.

GETTING THE STEAL

Throwing out base stealers requires arm strength, accuracy, and a quick release. Young catchers should learn the proper release and footwork first. Their arm strength and accuracy will develop with age and practice.

The actual throw to second base is what the fans notice, but your focus in practice should be on the mechanics that precede the throw. Get your rear end up in the air with a runner on first base. The baserunner is allowed to leave first base as the pitch is released, so a position player should yell out that the runner is stealing. If the runner is going, push off your back foot (right foot for right-handers, left for left-handers) to thrust your momentum forward. Catch the ball with two hands out in front of your body, and bring the ball directly back behind your ear. Do not drop your arm down by your side, as if you were throwing from the outfield. This takes too much time. Take a short step toward second base and throw.

Keep your throw low, like a line drive. A looping throw takes too much time to get to the base. If you cannot reach the base on a straight line, reach it on one bounce. If your arm is not strong enough to reach second base on one bounce, take an extra step before releasing the ball. This will allow you to get your whole body behind the throw.

Throw the ball to the first-base side of second base, not the shortstop side, and aim low (for your teammate's kneecaps) to put your middle infielder in good position to make a quick tag.

If you are trying to catch a runner stealing third, the principles are basically the same—line drive throw, second-base side of the bag, stay low, quick release, etc.—but you have the advantage of a shorter throw. The biggest difference, however, is that a right-handed batter will be in your way. Step in front of the batter, toward the fair-territory side. Extend your lead arm and push her out of the way if necessary. Practice throwing to third with a batter who does not get out of the way, just as if you were in a game situation.

If necessary, push the batter out of your way to make a clear path to throw the ball. According to the rules, you have the right to an unobstructed throw. If the batter fails to clear, she will be called out for interfering with you.

DEVELOPING A CATCHER'S INSTINCT

Calling pitches and directing the play are two vital areas of a catcher's game, and they can be learned only through experience. Rehearse calling out bases in practice so it becomes instinctual. During the game, you can review a small list of checkpoints to help you make a quick and accurate call. Ask yourself these questions before every pitch.

1. How many outs are there?
2. Where are the runners?
3. Who are the runners?
4. Who is at bat?

CATCHER'S TIP

Calling the game is the hardest thing for a catcher to learn. You do not have a lot of people coaching catchers at the high-school level, so a lot of catchers have to learn on their own. It is just something that you have to pick up from experience. It is not the way it should be, but a lot of people leave catching alone because they do not know what to do with it. In college, though, a good coach can really help out with that, and so can the pitchers. In college you really begin to learn different pitchers' strengths as well as batters' weaknesses, because everyone's scouting them and helping you out.

You can scout the batters by yourself, though. You remember what they did the last time they came to bat. You can do it when the batter's on deck, even. Watch their swing. How do they step? How do they swing? If they have an uppercut, you are going to want to be throwing the rise ball. If they step into the pitch, you want to be able to come inside. If they step away, you know the outside pitch will work. But it is not perfect. Sometimes batters show weaknesses, but they can also cover them, too, and you do not know. You take that chance when you attack them at the plate.

—Shelly Stokes

⑤ What is the score?

⑥ What is the count?

Only when you combine the answers to all six of these questions can you come up with the right call. Calling the right pitch can help dictate the action that will serve your team best. For instance, in an obvious bunt situation, call for a high pitch to make it difficult on the batter to bunt the ball on the ground. If a fly ball will score a run for the opposition, call for a drop pitch in hopes of getting a ground ball. By manipulating the pitch selection you may be able to influence the batter into producing the type of hit that works best for your team.

THE OUTFIELD

In game two of the 1996 Olympics against the Netherlands, U.S. pitcher Christa Williams was in a bit of a jam in the top of the first inning. With two outs and a runner on second base, a Netherlands batter stroked a line drive into right-center field that was destined to find the outfield grass. But before the

Netherlands could celebrate an early 1–0 lead, U.S. center fielder Laura Berg stretched out to make a spectacular, diving catch to thwart the opposition's rally. Berg's catch jump started the U.S. offense as they went on to win by a 9–0 score.

Though speed and agility played a major role in Berg making that great catch, other factors were also at play. Her positioning, anticipation, instinct, and judgment also assisted her in making the play. Without any one of those elements, the ball probably would have fallen in for a hit.

To become a good outfielder, initially focus your attention to one simple drill: Field hundreds upon hundreds of fly balls. By doing this you will develop judgment of fly balls. You can have the greatest speed and the best form of any outfielder in the world, but without good judgment those skills will be worthless. To judge the flight of the ball, the direction of its path, and where it will land, you have to see as many balls come off the bat as possible. With this you will also begin to develop confidence in your abilities. Once you have confidence in the outfield, you've achieved the most difficult task.

Batting practice is the best place to field fly balls. Balls come off the bat just as they will in the game. Treat every batting-practice hit as though it were in a game situation. When a coach hits balls to you, the flight of the ball is not quite the same, and since you know the ball is coming to you, it does not provide an accurate test of how quickly you are breaking on the ball. It's helpful, but not as much as fielding balls batted off live pitching.

Work on tracking down short tosses from your coach. This drill will build confidence in your ability to catch the ball on the run.

POSITIONING

Much like the positions in the infield, where you position yourself in the outfield depends on a number of factors. The score, number of outs, type of hitter, and baserunners all factor in to where you take the ready position in the outfield. Always pay attention to what the other two outfielders are doing. Regardless of whether you play left, right, or center field, communicate with the other

two oufielders. If the center fielder shades (moves over) toward the left-center-field gap, the right and left fielders should probably move that way as well. If the left fielder moves in shallow to defend against a possible slap hit, the center fielder should be aware of her position.

The best outfielder plays center field. If you are a center fielder, you must have a take-charge personality. Any ball you can get to is yours. You are responsible for covering as much territory as possible, and for calling off the other outfielders when necessary. It's your job to make sure the right and left fielders are in the correct position, and to back them up on every play.

The left fielder has to be very astute in knowing the skills of each hitter on the opposing team. Position yourself deep in the outfield when a power hitter is batting, and just behind the infield when a slap hitter is at the plate. Remind yourself of the game situation; that will help you to determine your starting spot in the outfield. All fly balls will carry either straight at you or toward the foul line. Balls off the bats of right-handed hitters tend to hook toward the line while those hit by left-handed hitters often produce a slice toward the foul line. Always back up throws to third base, and also throws to second base that come from the right side of the infield.

Right field is very similar to left field in that fly balls most commonly carry toward the foul line. It is extremely important to back up bases when you're playing right field. With the popularity of bunting and slap hitting, overthrows to first base occur with regularity. An alert right fielder can help minimize the damage of errant throws.

Get into the ready position on every pitch. The best fielders want the ball to be hit to them.

CATCHING THE FLY BALL

The ability to judge where the ball is going to come down is a major step toward becoming a good outfielder. The next step is taking the most direct route to that spot and catching the ball.

On every pitch to the plate, you should prepare by getting into the ready position. As an outfielder, the ready position requires bending slightly at the waist while standing with your feet shoulder-width apart. Take one step forward with your glove-side foot followed by a step with your throwing-side foot as the pitch is being delivered.

Backpedaling in the outfield is a cardinal sin.

—John Rittman, head coach, Stanford University

When a fly ball is hit to the outfield in your direction, take a split second to gauge the flight of the ball. Outfielders often attempt to get such a good jump that they react too quickly, causing them to misjudge the ball. Pay attention to how the ball is hit, and quickly process this information. Did it appear as if the ball came off the sweet spot of the bat, or did the batter get jammed (hit below the barrel)? Did the hitter time the pitch perfectly, or was she fooled and lunged out onto her front foot? Sometimes you can tell how well the ball was hit by the sound it makes off the bat. All of these clues can help you estimate the flight and the distance of the batted ball.

Fly balls that the outfielder has to travel back on are the most difficult to catch. First, you have to determine on which side of you the ball is hit. If it's over your right shoulder, take a drop step with your right foot. A drop step is the first step you take, and it

From the ready position, take a drop step to turn your body in the direction you need to run (30). If you're going to catch the ball over your left shoulder, drop your left foot back. Run in a straight line to where you think the ball will come down. Every five or six steps, look back to keep an eye on the ball (31). When you arrive at the spot where the ball will come down, turn around to face the ball. Catch the ball with two hands over your throwing-side shoulder. Take two steps and throw the ball back to infield or cut-off player.

opens up your body to run in the direction you've estimated the ball will land. On a ball that is hit over your right shoulder, swing your right foot open (to your right and behind you, as shown in Figure 31). This clears your hips and allows you to run directly to the spot.

After you have taken your drop step, take your eye off the ball, run to the target area (the spot where you believe the ball will land), and then find the ball again. Young outfielders commonly make the mistake of keeping their eye on the ball during its entire flight. This will cause you to drift. Drifting means that you're coasting along with the ball and not running at full speed.

When you get to the location of where the ball is coming down, find it and square up to face the infield. Catch the ball over your throwing shoulder with two hands. When you wait for the ball to come down, you may even want to take two or three steps back so your momentum is coming forward as you catch the ball. This helps you add power to your throw.

Always keep the wind conditions in mind. If you are playing right field with a wind blowing from left field across right field, balls are going to carry even stronger toward the foul line. If the wind is at your back (blowing in to home plate), it will knock down fly balls, and they will not travel as far.

CATCHING THE TEXAS LEAGUERS

Balls hit in the air that land behind the infielders but in front of the outfielders are called "Texas Leaguers." Outfielders have a much greater chance of catching Texas Leaguers because they are running in for the ball, and the infielders are chasing the ball over their head. If the fly ball is a short one, and if you are competing for it with the infielders, you are responsible for determining who gets it. If you can get to the ball, take charge and call them off. It is your ball to catch. When running for a ball, catch it with the fingers of your glove pointed toward the sky if it is above your waist. Anything below your waist, turn the glove over and make a "basket catch." Diving or sliding to catch the ball is a last resort. Many injuries are suffered by players who do not know the correct way to land. If the game is on the line, go for the spectacular catch. At other times, however, it may be a better idea to play it safe.

MAKING THE THROW

The fundamentals of throwing the ball in the infield are largely based on getting rid of the ball quickly. With longer throws from the outfield, however, you should take a little extra time in an effort to get a lot more power into your throw. You should also get rid of the ball as quickly as possible, but do not rush it so much that your throw suffers.

The toughest ball to judge as an outfielder is a line drive that's hit directly at you. In that situation, we teach to open up to the glove hand side and get turned one way or the other.

—John Rittman

The biggest difference is your arm swing. Instead of pulling the ball out of your glove and taking it directly behind your ear, drop your arm down by your waist to create a bigger arm circle. This generates more power on your throw, allowing the ball to carry a greater distance. Your follow-through should also be exaggerated. The longer follow-through enables you to make long throws on a line instead of a high arc. When you throw, bring your arm almost all the way down to your ankle at the end of the throw. The infield follow-through is about three-quarters of this.

If you can throw the ball to the base on a straight line, throw it directly to the bag. When throwing right to the base, err on the side of a low throw. An infielder has a chance to scoop a low throw. There is nothing she can do to field a throw over her head. Use a cutoff player if there is any arc in your throw. Two throws with good pace and velocity are faster than one long, looping throw. Hit your cutoff in the chest to give her an easy ball to   handle.

BACKING UP THE BASES

The pitcher is on the rubber poised for her next pitch. You're set in the ready position, prepared to make a game-saving catch in left field. With runners on first and second and nobody out, the opposing offense is threatening to chip away at your 2–0 lead. The pitch is delivered and it's hit on the ground back to the pitcher. Okay, now you can relax. Wrong! The pitcher may throw to third base, and it's your responsibility to back up the base.

Just because a ball is not hit to you in the outfield does not

To catch a ball below your waist, turn the glove over so the pocket faces the sky. Cover the ball with your throwing hand, find your target, and throw the ball.

I'm amazed at what poor throwing mechanics most outfielders have. I think a lot of times outfielders are left behind because if a college is going to hire a coach to have a specialty in some area, outfield is usually not the area they are thinking of.

—Teresa Wilson, head coach, University of Washington

mean the play is over for you. You are still involved in the game. The right fielder must always back up first base and back up second base when throws are coming from the left side of the field. She should also back up on balls hit to the center fielder. The left fielder always backs up third base and backs up second base when the throw is coming from the right side of the field. She also backs up the center fielder. The center fielder backs up throws to second base, and she backs up on balls hit to her two other outfielders. Keep your head in the game, and you may keep some unnecessary runs from scoring.

DRILL TIME

HIT, THEN BUNT

Line up players around third base or shortstop. Hit the first player in line a good, hard hit. She should field it and throw it to first. As she is throwing to first, drop a bunt in front of the plate. This fielder then must recover and scramble in to get that, which she also fields and throws to first. She goes to the end of the line, and the next player is up. Have a catcher at the plate with you to get the balls back from the first baseman.

TAG

For this drill, divide your team into groups of four, five, or six. Set up two "bases" for each group, base A and base B. Two or three players from each group should be at base A and an equal number at base B. Players are in a relay race while learning how to make the tag correctly by immediately placing the glove on the ground.

The ball starts at base A. The whistle blows, and the player with the ball throws it to the first player in line at base B. Her teammate receives it and immediately touches the ground in front of the bag, as she should in a game. Then she straightens up and throws it back to the next person at base A. She then follows her throw (very quickly if there are only four players in a group) and gets in line at base A. When a player at base A has made a throw, she runs and gets in line at base B. When a player ends up in her original position, she sits down. The first team to complete the circuit wins.

TWO ON TWO

This is an excellent fielding drill because it works on fielding ground balls and also teaches players how to work together as a unit. Set up two cones about twenty feet apart. Two players are a team and set up between the cones. Two other players are the hitting team. They take turns trying to hit the balls (self-tossing) through the cones, while the two fielders do their best to prevent them. The fielders stay in place until the hitters get a ball through and then they switch places. If you want to make it more of a competition, players can count how many balls they've stopped and pairs rotate so that they are not always playing against the same people.

FLY BALL FUN

This drill combines good fly ball fielding skills with conditioning. You need an infielder at each base, and three fungo hitters. The rest of the team lines up on the left field foul line. The first hit goes to left field, and the first player in line goes to field it. She throws it to third and sprints to center field where she should be receiving the next ball. She throws that to second base and runs to right field to get her third hit, she throws to first base. She then jogs back to the end of the line in left field. Because there are three infielders and three fungo hitters, three fielders can be going at once. As soon as the first player has caught the ball, the first fungo hitter should hit another one for the next player in line, and so on.

U.S. Olympic team infielder Julie Smith throws to first base to complete a double play.

DEFENSIVE STRATEGIES

Because there are several different ways to score a run or runs, offenses develop strategies to generate maximum run production. It is the obligation of the defense to counter those attacks with strategies of their own. Some offenses rely on power, others on speed, and the best teams rely on a combination of both. It's up to the defense to recognize the offensive system of attack and to counter it with a strategy of their own. Remember, softball (along with baseball) is a unique sport because the defending team controls the ball. In other sports, the team attacking holds the ball in their possession. Thus in softball the defense is in a unique position to control play.

Before developing complicated defensive strategies, coaches have to make sure their players know the basics of defense and are mentally tuned into the game. Complicated defenses will not work if the players do not have the skills to execute them. Imagine trying to teach beginners how to execute a good rundown defense when they have not yet mastered throwing and catching.

On defense you have to be focused on the task at hand. Unlike hitting or throwing, you cannot execute defensive plays by relying

Softball is a unique sport in that the defense starts with the ball and can largely dictate what the offense can do.

on muscle, memory, and instinct. Each situation is different. On every pitch you will have designated responsibilities specific to your position. A breakdown by any individual on defense—poor positioning, failure to back up a base, throwing to the wrong base—can result in a big inning for the opposition.

A runner on second base dictates that the bunt may be in order. The defense must be drilled on how to defend this play.

DEFENDING THE BUNT

Any time there is a runner on base and fewer than two outs, prepare for the bunt. Each player has a specific responsibility when defending against the bunt. Pitchers should throw the ball high in the strike zone in an attempt to induce the hitter to pop the ball up in the air. The third baseman and the first baseman should move to a position between one-third and halfway to home plate. The second baseman must be prepared to cover first base and the shortstop to cover second base. With a runner on second base, the shortstop must cover third base if the third baseman is charging in to field the bunt.

Outfielders must stay alert and back up bases. The right fielder is the backup on all throws to first and on throws to second base from the left side of the infield. The center fielder should back up all throws to second base, and the left fielder backs up all throws to third base and throws to second base from the right side of the infield.

Before you can get into the defensive strategies that affect the game, you have to be mentally tuned into the game. You cannot use the strategies if you cannot focus. The mental game is part of defense, and if you do not have that, you are going to lose.

—Ralph Weekly, coach of the national team and head coach, University of Tennessee, Chattanooga

3

The first baseman has aggressively fielded this bunt and is in excellent position to make an out.

We want catchers to feel that every bunt is theirs, but, of course, we're also saying that to the corners.

*—Cindy Cohen,
head coach,
Princeton University*

The pitcher and the catcher must be prepared to field the bunt aggressively. The catcher should field any ball she can reach because she is facing the field and has the best view of the play as it develops. Any throw is much easier for her. If she does not field the bunt, she needs to call out who should field the ball and to which base the ball should be thrown. The pitcher is required to field bunts as well. A good-fielding pitcher and catcher can make a team very difficult to bunt against.

Practice bunt defense as a team (including the pitcher and the catcher) because all the players have to work together and know who is going to cover what area. The first baseman should only field balls that are coming right down her line, because she has to turn her body more than anyone else to throw to first or second base. If the ball is bunted toward the middle of the infield, the third baseman should make the play because she will have the easiest throw. With a runner on first base, the pitcher immediately covers third base if the third baseman fields the ball. This keeps the lead runner from rounding second base and advancing to third base. Because the shortstop is covering second base, third base is initially left vacant.

The catcher evaluates the runner going to second (or third) and calls out where the ball is to be thrown before anyone retrieves the ball. If she is the one fielding the ball, then the shortstop makes the call. In every bunt situation, make it your goal to retire the lead runner. But when in doubt, get the sure out at first base. There are only so many outs in a game, so take them whenever your opponent gives them.

F I E L D E R ' S   T I P

Because many bunted balls travel near the third-base line or first-base line, all fielders should know exactly how far away the foul line is, relative to their position. The foul line often proves to be a fielder's best ally.

Since the first baseman and the third baseman are positioned near the foul line when defending against the bunt, any ball bunted toward their outside shoulder has a good chance of rolling foul and becoming a strike. Any bunted ball near the foul line that requires a fielder to make a difficult play should be allowed to roll foul. This is especially true when the batter attempts a two-strike bunt. Using the foul line to your advantage makes it much more difficult for the batter to execute a successful bunt.

The best method of fielding a bunt is called a shovel or a scoop. Instead of opening your glove and allowing the ball to roll in, keep your glove closed, and use it to push or "shovel" the ball into your throwing hand. Stay low to the ground when making the throw. Standing up will slow you down.

You can pick the ball up with your bare hand, but this technique does not save enough time to make it worth the risk of not getting a good grip on the ball or losing the ball entirely. The bare-hand pickup should be used only for balls that have stopped or almost stopped.

DEFENDING THE SLAP

When a left-handed hitter steps up to the plate, sirens should go off in your head. Any left-handed hitter is a threat to slap-hit, especially one who has good running speed. Most often, slap hitters attempt to hit into the hole between third base and shortstop. The slapper is trying to create a running race with the first baseman, so the slapper will not want to put the ball on the right side of the field. Adjust your positioning accordingly.

The third baseman should move up about halfway to the plate. The shortstop should cheat (move) over toward third base and move in a little until she is just behind the base path. The first baseman positions herself according to the speed of the slapper, moving farther back against a faster runner. The outfield should play shallow (a few steps behind the infield dirt) and fill in the gaps created by the infield.

The shortstop has a difficult play to make because she normally has to charge the ball to make the play. With a runner on first base, the situation becomes even more complex. On a ball hit to her, the shortstop has to decide whether to throw to first base

Everything you want to do in a sacrifice bunt situation is aimed at getting that lead runner out. If you do it right, you will be able to get that lead runner 90 percent of the time—plus the runner at first, too.

—Sheila Cornell Douty,
player,
U.S. Olympic team

The best defense against slappers is to not let those slappers hit the ball. We identify their weaknesses and pitch to them.

—Ken Erickson,
head coach,
University of South Florida

On the national team, the positioning of third and first depends on who we have on the mound. If we have Lisa Fernandez on the mound, then the corners can be wide. If we have Michelle Granger, then they are going to have to push in a bit. She is a great pitcher but not known for her defense as much.

—Ralph Weekly

The classic defense against the slap hitter: The third baseman is playing halfway between home plate and third base, the shortstop is playing in and toward third base, and the left fielder is stationed just beyond the infield dirt.

or to second base, and on balls hit to the pitcher or to the right side of the infield, she has to break for second base. This may be easy for great shortstops such as Dot Richardson or Jennifer McFalls, but average high-school and college shortstops struggle with this play. With a runner on second base, the shortstop has to cover third base on balls hit to the third baseman. Do everything in your power to keep the runner from reaching third base.

PREPARE IN PRACTICE

Practice defending against the slap by re-creating the situation. Put a runner in the batter's box, tell her to run toward first, and then roll the ball onto the field. This is much more efficient than having a batter attempt to place slap hits. Unless the ball is hit directly at her, the pitcher should not be fielding slap hits.

At advanced levels of play, there are good slap hitters who can also hit the ball with authority. This type of hitter causes headaches. The best way to defend against her is to first pay close attention to the game situation. Is it early or late in the game? What's the score? Are there runners on base? How many outs are there? What is the count? In general, it's best to play in a little, defending against the slap, but not so much that she's able to stroke the ball past you with ease. See if you can detect anything in her stance or how she's holding her hands that may tip off what she is doing. If she's way back in the batter's box, or if her back foot is turned toward the pitcher, she may be preparing to slap-hit.

THE SQUEEZE PLAY

To successfully defend against the squeeze bunt, you need to detect it before it happens. Without early detection it is nearly impossible to defend against a properly executed squeeze play. By anticipating the play you can call for a pitchout. The hitter will not be able to connect with the ball, and the runner from third will be an easy out.

Look for any clue that the squeeze may be on. Inexperienced coaches often flash no signs down at third base with a runner on third. If you notice the coach suddenly flashing a sign to the hitter, act on your suspicion. Another way to pick up that a squeeze play has been called is by looking at the batter and the runner on third base. In most cases the batter and the runner will have to give a sign back to the coach to confirm that they know the squeeze play is on. If the runner or the batter fails to give the countersign, the play is off. Knowing all this, look for the countersign from the batter or the runner. The batter may touch the top of her helmet, tap her cleats with her bat, or grab the barrel of the bat with her hand. Anything that looks suspicious or out of the ordinary could be an indication that the squeeze play is on.

If they do catch you off guard, however, the only chance at getting the runner at the plate is to barehand the ball and flip it to the catcher in one motion. Field the ball out in front of your throwing foot so you can step and toss at the same time. Do not

To defend the squeeze play, the third baseman must alert the catcher, pitcher and infielders that the runner at third is breaking for home. Most teams have the third baseman yell, "Squeeze!" as soon as the runner breaks.

break your wrist; it must be stiff so the ball will stay flat. Stay low to the ground while throwing. Generally, though, you'll be throwing the ball to first for the sure out.

TEXAS LEAGUERS

A Texas Leaguer is a short hit that goes over the infield but not far enough to reach the outfield. This "bloop" hit poses problems for the defense because the ball is placed into an area where it could be caught by several fielders, or by none at all. The proximity of so many fielders chasing the ball can be dangerous. Serious collisions are not uncommon. The key to catching the Texas Leaguer is good communication.

Here's a good drill for working on your communication. Standing on the pitcher's mound, the coach throws the ball into the air between the infielder and outfielders, simulating a Texas Leaguer. Both the infielders and the outfielders should hustle to catch the ball. There are clear-cut rules to this play. The outfielder makes the catch without question if she calls for the ball. Once she calls for the ball, the infielders should immediately veer out of the way. When calling for the ball, repeatedly yell out, "Mine! Mine! Mine! Mine!"

Infielders should call for any ball that they can easily reach and catch without turning their back to the infield. Regardless of who attempts to make the play, you have to call for the ball loudly and clearly, over and over, "Mine! Mine! Mine! Mine!" If your name is Mary, the other infielders and outfielder should then yell, "Mary! Mary! Mary! Mary!" In that way there is no confusion over whose ball it is to catch.

When playing middle infield, you must act just like an outfielder to get back for that type of pop fly. Take a drop step—right or left, depending on which shoulder it's over—tuck your glove, and run. Take quick glances back at the ball to make sure you're running in the right direction. Do not drift back to the ball. Continue running until you're called off. If you are not called off, make the catch.

Remember: Everyone should aggressively pursue the ball; outfielders should take any ball they can reach; communicate with one another loudly and clearly.

PICKOFFS

At times, baserunners get lazy or overconfident. Sometimes they just plain don't pay attention. If you notice this happening, get the attention of the catcher and signal for a pickoff. The signal can be as simple as tugging at your jersey or grabbing dirt from the infield and tossing it. The catcher, whom you have already made eye

I'm a shortstop. I'm greedy. I'm going to find the best way to get to that Texas leaguer, but my left fielder is in control. If she calls it one time, I gotta get out of there, whether she is going to get there or not.

*—Jennifer McFalls,
player,
U.S. national team*

contact with, should then give a countersign. This might be a tug of the mask or touching the heel of her shoe with her throwing hand. As the pitch passes the batter, break quietly behind the runner to the base. The catcher should throw the ball immediately after she receives it. Time the play so you arrive at the base just before the ball gets there. If you break too early, you may alert the runner.

A planned pickoff play to first base is very effective in bunt situations. This play is specifically designed for when a right-handed batter is at the plate. The pitcher, catcher, and first baseman all must be aware that a pickoff play is on. The catcher sends a sign to the first baseman, and the first baseman relays the countersign. The catcher then calls for a pitchout. The first baseman begins to creep toward home plate as the pitcher winds up. When the pitcher releases the ball, the baserunner begins to shuffle off first base and prepares to break for second on the bunt. The first baseman then retreats back to first base as the pitch is released. As the catcher receives the ball, she immediately fires a throw down to first base.

This play is so effective because the baserunner is anticipating a bunt. Her job is to see the ball hit the ground and then take off for second as fast as she can. When she sees the hitter square around, instinct tells her to shuffle off the base farther than normal to make sure she gets a good jump. That's when you nail her.

FIRST AND THIRD

With runners on first and third bases, the offense is presented with an opportunity to manufacture a run without the batter swinging. The runner on first will attempt to steal second base on the pitch. When the catcher throws to second to get the out, the runner on third base breaks for home. This is called a double steal, and it is a difficult play to defend against. The middle infielder receiving the throw from the catcher has to decide whether she should catch the ball and tag the runner out, or cut the ball off and throw home. If the defense makes even one error in judgment or physical execution, the run will score.

There are several ways to handle this play on defense, but you first must decide how important that run is on third base. If you're ahead by a lot of runs, try to get the out at second base; but in a close game, you can't afford to allow that runner to score.

The most common way to defend against the first-and-third situation is to have the catcher throw the ball straight through to second base. The shortstop positions herself in front of the bag at second base. If the runner on third breaks for home as the catcher releases the ball, the second and third basemen should yell, "Four! Four! Four!" The shortstop should come off the bag (toward home plate), cut the ball off, and immediately throw home. If the

The one thing we try not to do is give a runner a base. Your personnel are going to dictate what you are going to do. If you have a good catcher with a strong arm and good middle infielders, there are a lot more options.

—Mike Candrea, head coach, University of Arizona

U.S. Olympic team catcher Gillian Boxx puts the tag on China's Chunfang Zang during the third inning of the 1996 Olympic gold medal game. Zhang attempted to steal home on a first and third play, but was thrown out at the plate. The U.S. went on to win the game 3–1.

You know what the key is to the first-and-third? Do it right the first time and no one will run it on you again.

—Ralph Weekly

runner stays at third base, the shortstop receives the throw at the base to tag out the runner attempting to steal. A variation to this play is to have the second baseman stand in front of the shortstop. If the runner breaks from third, the second baseman cuts the ball off and throws home. If the runner stays at third, the second baseman allows the ball go through to the shortstop.

Another method of defense is to have the catcher fake a throw to second base and then throw directly to third base. Faking the throw will lure the runner on third base into breaking for home. With her momentum going toward home plate, the runner will have trouble getting back to third. The third baseman must make sure she gives a clear target for the catcher to throw to. Stand to the second-base side of third base to ensure a clear throwing lane.

Another trick is to have the catcher throw the ball right back to the pitcher. The catcher should use the same throwing motion as if she were throwing through to second base, but the pitcher intercepts the throw. If the runner at third is aggressive, you may catch her jumping too far off the base. The pitcher can then throw to third or run straight at the baserunner, forcing her to run home or back to third.

Practice this situation as much as possible. Proper execution may get you a critical out. Failure to execute the first-and-third defense means that the offense will become more aggressive, putting pressure on you at every opportunity. Shut them down, though, and they may take a more conservative approach.

The key to quickly tagging the baserunner during a rundown is getting her to commit to a base. Put pressure on the runner immediately. If you allow her to dance around in the middle of the basepaths, you're risking an error each time the ball changes hands.

RUNDOWNS

It is very frustrating when you execute a perfect first-and-third play and then blow something as simple as a rundown. Rundowns occur when a player is caught between two bases. In first-and-third situations, the runner from first base will often purposely get caught in a rundown just to give the runner at third base an opportunity to score. The goal for the defense is to tag the runner out quickly, using the fewest amount of throws possible.

When you are holding the ball, your job is to run hard at the baserunner. If you can catch up to her before she gets to the base she is running to, tag her out. If not, at least make her run hard and commit to a base. Run hard with the ball held up by your ear so your teammate (standing at the base) can see it. As the runner gets close to the bag (twenty feet), flip the ball to your teammate. Because the baserunner is running hard, she will not be able to stop and run in the opposite direction to prolong the rundown. Your teammate should catch the ball and tag her out with ease.

If you are the player standing on the base awaiting the throw, make sure your teammate with the ball has a clear throwing lane. Do not stand in the line of the runner. Once the runner gets close enough (about twenty feet), call out, "Ball!" This signals your teammate to deliver the ball to you. If the runner attempts to slide into the base, stay on the bag and tag her out. If she tries to stop and change direction, catch the ball with your momentum moving forward and tag her out.

Here are a few basic rules for rundowns:

1 Your hand should always stay in the three-fourths cocked position, up by the ear, so you do not have to go into a major windup to throw the ball.

2 Be on the same side of the base path as your other fielder.

3 Communicate with a short word such as "Ball!" when you want the ball thrown to you.

4 Force the baserunner to make a commitment; run her hard to a base.

5 Have as few throws as possible.

6 Fielders not involved in the rundown should back up other fielders. Don't get caught standing around.

The best drill to use for a rundown is a five-person drill using rubber balls and no gloves. This really helps the players learn to do this accurately. One girl starts in the middle of the two bases, and the fielder with the ball initiates the rundown by running right at her. As soon as the runner is tagged out, she goes to the end of the line.

RELAYS AND CUTS

When a ball is hit deep into the outfield, the middle infielders need to move out to provide cut offs for the outfielders. The shortstop is the cutoff (relay) on balls hit to the left of second base, and the second baseman is the cutoff (relay) for balls hit to the right of second base. Most outfielders are unable to make a strong throw to a base from an outfield fence. The middle infielders cut the distance of the outfielder's throw nearly in half. Two strong throws are more productive than one long and weak throw.

Whichever middle infielder is not taking the cutoff throw must back up the cutoff in case of an errant throw. This is called the trailer. Follow her out and make sure she is lined up with the outfielder and the base she is throwing to. Watch what the baserunners are doing so you can tell your teammate where to throw the ball when she catches it.

If you're the cutoff player, hold your arms up in the air to provide the outfielder with a target. As the ball is in flight, open your left leg toward the infield to get into throwing position. Listen to the trailer for directions on where to throw the ball. Receive the throw, turn to the base, and throw.

On base hits to left field with a runner on second base, the third baseman becomes the cutoff player for the outfielder. The first baseman is the cutoff for balls hit to center field and to right field.

My first year at Georgia Tech, we were playing a game I'll never forget. My team had a 2–1 lead in the seventh inning, and they had a runner on second with one out. They hit a ground ball up the middle. Just one of those hits that short and second cannot get to. The ball rolls through and the run scores. But . . . on the play to home we blew the cutoff play. The runner went to second. The next batter hit another one right up the middle and scored the runner who should never have been on second in the first place. Since then, I've incorporated that cutoff play into my practices, and I haven't had it happen to me again.

—*Ralph Weekly*

The outfield relay play. In this case, the outfielder throws the ball to the first baseman who catches it and delivers it to the catcher.

The cut happens when the catcher sees that the throw to home—whether from an outfielder or a relay—is going to be too late or off line. She will yell, "Cut!" and then give directions on whether to hold the ball or throw to another base.

It is the catcher's responsibility to line up the cutoff player on a direct line between her and the outfielder. She will call out, "One step to the left!" or "Two steps to the right!" Once the ball is thrown from the outfield, she will decide where the ball goes. If she says nothing, the cutoff player does not touch the ball; she lets it go through. The catcher must be decisive and yell loudly and clearly so everyone can hear her.

DRILL TIME

CUTOFF DRILL

Players in the cutoff position must feel comfortable receiving the throw and getting rid of it quickly. Here is a drill for improving your accuracy and speed of delivery. Line your infielders up in a straight line in the outfield. Every player should be about sixty feet apart, with their backs to home plate. Start the ball at one end of the line. The first player throws the ball to the second player in line. She catches the ball on her glove side and relays the ball to the next player. This continues all the way down the line. When the ball gets to the end, turn around and relay the ball all the way back. If you have enough players, form two lines and make it a race.

GETTING STARTED

First Steps in Hitting a Softball

Here's how to get started in learning how to hit a softball. It's fun and its simple. Use your backyard, open sandlot or playground space, or softball field.

What you'll need:
❶ softballs ❷ softball bat ❸ rolled-up socks ❹ batting tee

Proper Grip

Before you actually start swinging, you'll need to learn how to take the proper grip. Place the bat on the ground between your legs with the handle closest to you (at 6 o'clock). Lean over, pick up the bat (Figure 1) and lift it directly over your hitting shoulder. Align the knuckles of your top hand somewhere between the second knuckles and back knuckles of the bottom

hand (Figure 2). Keep the bat more in the fingers of the top hand and not deep in the palm.

Proper Stance

Square you feet and spread them slightly more than shoulder-width apart (Figure 3). Bend at the knees and push down on the inside of the balls of your feet. Keep your weight evenly distributed and muscles slightly tense. This is the athletic position. Next raise your hands up as if you are taking a stance (Figure 4). Shift the weight slightly to the back side keeping pressure on the instep and ball of the rear foot (so that the weight does not roll onto the outside of the foot). Put a bat in your hands (Figure 5) and shift

back a little more until you feel comfortable. Next imagine a ball coming over the plate, rock your weight back (pressing down with the ball of your rear foot), step and swing as hard as you can.

HITTING OFF A TEE

Here you can focus on stride, swing and follow-through. In Figure 6 the hitter shows good form. Her hips are turned, the bat is level and her head is down, eyes focusing on the ball.

IMPROVING EYE-HAND COORDINATION

To improve your timing and eye-hand coordination, practice hitting slowly tossed rolled up socks. Have the pitcher toss the socks into various parts of the strike zone (Figure 7). When you take pitches that are out of the strike zone, call out the pitch location, such as "Low and outside." This will help you learn the strike zone.

GETTING STARTED

First Steps in Throwing and Catching a Softball

Here's how to get started in learning how to throw and catch a softball. Use your backyard, open sandlot or playground space, or softball field (Figure 8).

What you'll need:
1 softball **2** gloves

PROPER GRIP

Grasp the ball with three fingers across the widest part of the ball, placing the thumb and pinkie finger alongside and under the ball to give it support (Figures 8 and 9). Keep the ball resting as much as possible in the fingers and not in the palm. Apply thumb pressure on the ball with the tip or thumb pad (opposite side of the nail). Do not slide the ball back and down toward

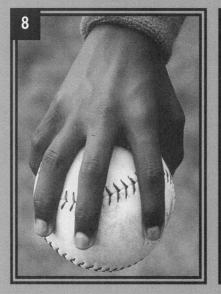

the second joint, which is closest to the palm. Note: Taking the proper grip will be easier if your hands are large. Gripping the ball with smaller hands will cause more of the ball to rest in your palm. Don't fret—you will still be able to throw it with reasonable control, accuracy and speed. However, later when your hands have grown and you are able to grip more of the ball in your fingertips, you will add more snap, speed and spin to your throws.

PROPER THROWING MOTION

Shift your weight to your back leg, rotating the hips away from the target (Figure 10). Separate your hands, take the ball out of your glove, bring the ball back and up

(Figure 11). Step forward with your front foot, shifting your weight from the rear foot to the front foot, and extend your arm upward toward an imaginary 11 o'clock position (Figure 12). Lead the arm motion with the elbow. As you approach the 11 o'clock position move your arm and hand forward quickly and release the ball at the highest point, snapping your lower arm and wrist just as it passes an imaginary line extending from your ear skyward. Finish the throw by moving your arm down and across your body, thus following an imaginary diagonal from the throwing shoulder to the opposite knee.

CATCHING THE BALL

Catch the ball using both hands. Snag the ball with your glove, bring your free hand around to the front heel area of the glove and press the ball back into the pocket as it hits the pocket or webbing (Figures 13 and 14).

PITCHING

8

THE FUNDAMENTALS OF PITCHING

I f you are to learn only one thing from this book, let it be this: Pitching is the single-most important aspect of the game. Dominant pitching can transform a good team into champions. As the old adage says, good pitching will stop good hitting any day.

Good pitching will beat good hitting every time.

In 1998, the NCAA Division I softball national championship came down to one game between the defending champion Arizona Wildcats and the Fresno State Bulldogs. Fresno State had an outstanding pitcher in Amanda Scott, who entered the game with a 23–4 record. Arizona countered with pitching star Nancy Evans, who boasted an unblemished 36–0 record going into the final game. The Wildcats had not given up a run during their World Series run in Oklahoma City, outscoring their opponents 64–0.

The championship game lived up to its billing as the quintessential pitchers' duel. Both teams were scoreless through five innings. Fresno State threatened to score several times, but Evans performed at her best under pressure. Finally, the Wildcats' Nina Lindenberg stroked a solo home run over the left-field fence to give Fresno State a 1–0 lead in the bottom of the sixth inning. Scott retired the Arizona hitters on three straight groundouts in the final inning, giving Fresno State its first national championship.

Fresno State University team members celebrate their 1–0 victory over Arizona in the 1998 NCAA Division I softball national championship game.

PITCHING DICTATES THE GAME

You must have solid defense, timely hitting, and savvy base-running to win games, but when your pitching can limit the opposition to few or no runs, you will keep your team in every game, and this takes pressure off the offense. The 1996 gold-medal-winning Olympic softball team had outstanding offensive players, but their pitching carried them to the top. They defeated Puerto Rico, 10–0; the Netherlands, 9–0; Japan, 6–1; Chinese Taipei, 4–0; and Canada, 4–2; then lost to Australia, 2–1. They came back to defeat China three times: 3–2; 1–0 in eleven innings, and 3–1 in the final game. The pitching staff, led by Lisa Fernandez, Michele Granger, Michele Smith, Christa Williams, and Lori Harrigan, was nothing short of spectacular in leading the United States to the gold medal. In nine games they allowed just eight runs (six earned), ten walks, and twenty-eight hits. It's tough to lose games with pitching like that.

The pitcher sets the tempo of the game. If the pitcher is having trouble throwing strikes, or if opposing hitters are batting her pitches all over the field, fielders lose focus and the defense suffers. If she's throwing strike after strike and recording outs at a quick rate, her teammates stay alert and focused. If you are the type of player who enjoys the pressure of having the outcome of the game in your hands, the pitcher's mound is the place for you.

A pitcher is only a thrower until she learns to think. Once you learn to think, then you've become a pitcher.

—Teresa Wilson, head coach, University of Washington

Becoming a good pitcher requires commitment and focus. You must learn the proper fundamentals and consistently strive to perfect your craft. The best pitchers feature exceptional velocity, pinpoint control, and deception.

Pitchers who are practiced in the art of deception throw pitches that rise and drop, or that move into or away from the hitter. They also frequently change the speed of their pitches. Deception brings the mental aspect into the competitive mix; outstanding pitchers recognize that getting out batters is not just a physical contest.

When University of Arizona pitcher Nancy Evans threw a fastball on the inside corner that Fresno State's Nina Lindenberg blasted for the game-winning home run in the 1998 national championship game, she failed to use deception. Evans had fallen into a pattern of pitches to Lindenberg, who recognized it and made an adjustment (she "sat on," or anticipated, the pitch). After the game, Lindenberg commented that she anticipated Evans throwing her that pitch. "She threw it to me all year," Lindenberg said. "It was time for me to send one over, and she came with it [the inside fastball]." Lindenberg is a great hitter and Evans is a great pitcher, but Evans failed because of a mental lapse. She failed to keep the hitter guessing and off-balance.

> *The most important thing for a pitcher is to have a good, sound base in the fundamentals. You want a nice, balanced delivery. This should go from the start through the delivery through the follow-through.*
>
> *—Jay Miller, head coach, University of Missouri*

THE VELOCITY VS. CONTROL DEBATE

Coaching opinion differs on whether young pitchers should focus their initial efforts on developing control or learning to generate maximum velocity. However, we believe that the best results come from first learning how to generate maximum speed on your pitches, then focusing on controlling the ball. Many of the world's best golf instructors use this same approach with young golfers. They first teach youngsters to hit the ball as far as they can, coaching only the rudiments of proper swing mechanics, then later teach developing players how to direct and control their shots.

Because junior high, high school, and youth league coaches are often more interested in overall performance (won-and-lost record) of their team rather than individual development, they emphasize pitchers throwing strikes instead of increasing velocity. Coaches are not wrong for stressing this approach. Their job as the coach is to do what's best for the team, and the best way to achieve team success is to have a pitcher who throws the ball over the plate. As a team member your job is to do what is asked of you. But if you want to reach your potential as a pitcher, you must practice and develop your velocity on your own time. This includes practicing your pitching year-round.

Once you are throwing the ball with maximum velocity, you should begin working on controlling the location of your pitches. Maintain the same motion and practice until you can make the ball go where you want it to go. Do not get discouraged if your control does not evolve immediately. Learning the art of pitching does not happen overnight.

One good drill for improving control starts with drawing a large strike zone—two feet wide by three feet high—on a wall. Pitch to that strike zone until you can hit it consistently. Then make the rectangle smaller. Then put a circle in the rectangle. When you are able to consistently throw the ball inside that circle, focus your attention to the outline of the circle. Move the circle around the rectangle. This helps you to place your pitches on the edges of the strike zone. A lot of hitters can hit pitches that are in the middle of the strike zone, but few make solid contact with pitches on the corners of the strike zone.

Pacifica High School pitching star Amanda Freed displays the form that produces a 64 mile-per-hour rising fastball. Freed was named the 1998 Gatorade Circle of Champions National High School Softball Player of the Year by Scholastic Coach *magazine.*

PITCHER'S TIP

You have to practice and work to become a pitcher. The more innings you can pitch, the more control you will have. You cannot get in there and pitch until you have proper mechanics. That's the first thing you want to work on. Everyone who has developed into a great pitcher went through the stage where they walked more people than they struck out. They hit more batters than they struck out. It's part of the natural development of a pitcher. You never want to slow your motion to achieve control. There is a tendency to do that at first, but you hope that your coach won't allow you to do that because you will never develop into a great pitcher if that happens.

—Jay Miller

THE WINDMILL PITCH

The windmill method of throwing is today's universal pitching style. This is an underhand motion (required in fast-pitch softball) in which the pitching arm begins in front of the pitcher's body and then moves in a perfect circle backward and forward again until the ball is released at the hip. It produces power by using centrifugal force. Centrifugal force is the force created by the arm rotating outward or away from the axis (your body). To gain an understanding of the power of centrifugal force, hold a softball in your pitching hand down by your hip. Without any backswing, toss the ball (underhand) as far as you can. Now, from the same position, swing your arm (fully extended) in a clockwise circle before releasing. The ball will travel a much greater distance. This is a result of using centrifugal force.

The arm is like the propeller of a helicopter on its side.

— Lisa Fernandez,
pitcher, U.S. Olympic team

4

The windmill involves the entire body. It is not just an arm swing, because your arm by itself simply does not have the power necessary to move the ball fast enough. To generate arm speed you use the lower body, just as in hitting. Stride forward. This establishes a wide base. Then begin your forward weight shift by pushing off the pitching rubber; and continue the shift until you straighten the front leg. Rotate around your front leg; your belly button should face the batter. (All of this information will be covered in detail later in this chapter.)

Because the windmill utilizes both the lower and the upper half of your body, only repetitious training will enable you to establish correct form and a comfortable rhythm. For explanation and easier understanding, we've broken down the pitch into eight parts: the pitch presentation, the windup, the stride, the sideways rotation, the firm front side, the drag, the release, and the follow-through. Some of them happen simultaneously, and together they take but an instant. Be aware of each element, but be careful not to devote too much attention to one at the expense of others.

The windmill delivery is the most popular style of pitching today.

In years past, another type of motion, called the slingshot pitch, was also popular and used extremely effectively by pitchers such as Joan Joyce and Sandy Fischer, but the pitch has lost favor in the past few decades. "I think the reason the slingshot disappeared is that the timing had to be so perfect it was harder to break down," surmises pitcher and Washington coach Teresa Wilson. "And people generally feel, I guess, that the windmill is a more continuous motion, a more fluid motion, so that you could build up a little more momentum. You probably can throw harder with the slingshot, but it is too difficult to teach."

The slingshot pitch involved a sideways rotation of the body, while the arm moved backward until it was fully extended up toward the sky, with the wrist cocked. Then the pitcher stepped forward and snapped the arm downward, and then shifted the weight to the front foot, squaring up on the follow-through.

THE PITCH PRESENTATION

The pitch presentation begins with a sound grip on the softball and a comfortable stance on the pitching rubber. Your stance should remain the same on every pitch, but your grip will change depending on what type of pitch you are preparing to throw. (Different types of grips and pitches will be covered in Chapter 9.) For now we will focus on the fastball grip.

THE GRIP

Grip the softball with three fingers. Your middle three fingers lay across or with the seams, with the pinkie and your thumb on the sides of the ball. Hold the ball with your fingers, not your hand. Tucking the pinkie along the side ensures that the ball is not sitting back in your palm. Grip the ball so the fingers are the only part of your hand in contact with the ball (see Figure 5); otherwise, you will never get the proper snap upon release. As your hands grow and get stronger, you may want to try a two-fingered grip. Gripping with two fingers will increase the velocity of your pitch, but you may sacrifice some control.

For the fastball, hold the ball firmly but without too much pressure. Squeezing the ball too hard will tighten up your muscles in the hand, wrist, and forearm. Tension hinders your wrist snap, thereby decreasing the speed and movement of your pitch. Pitchers grip the ball across the seams or with them, whichever is more comfortable.

Gripping across the seams is called a four-seam pitch. When you release the ball using this grip, all four seams are rotating

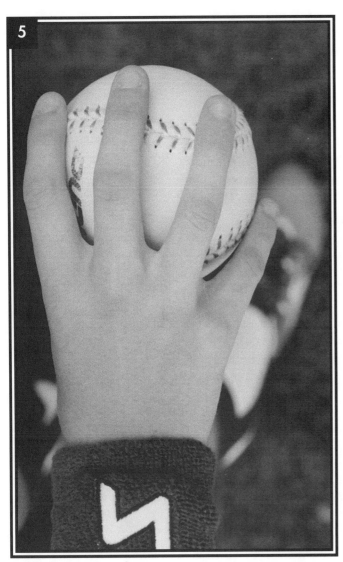

5

This is the grip for a four-seam fastball. Hold the ball across the seams and loose in your fingers to achieve maximum velocity.

perpendicular to the ball's path to the plate. It involves holding the ball so the seams facing you look like a C. Place your three middle fingers across that C. A four-seam pitch allows you to throw the ball straighter and faster. If you turn the ball and grip it with the seam (lay your fingers along the seams), you have a two-seam pitch. When you look at the ball now, the seams create a "U" shape. With this grip, only two seams are visible to the hitter. When you throw a two-seam pitch, this creates more sideward and downward movement on the ball as it travels to the plate. Resisting air currents are running signifcantly more across a smoother surface (fewer seams) and influence the path of the ball, giving it movement. Remember: Four seams for increased velocity, two seams for better movement.

You can also detect any flaws in your motion by paying attention to how the seams behave during a pitch's flight. Ask your catcher to pay attention to the spin on your pitches. When you are throwing a straight pitch, the seams should roll directly over one another. If they are turning to the side, chances are that you are releasing the ball with a twist in your wrist.

THE STANCE

The stance is the second element of the pitch presentation. Face the catcher with your hand on the ball and with the ball in your glove, resting in front of you. In effect, you are "presenting" the ball. Your arms should be about waist high, with your elbows at about a ninety-degree angle. Some pitchers like to hold the ball out of their glove and alongside their hip. This is fine as long as you are not tipping off your pitch by showing your grip to the batter. To avoid this, change your grip as you put the ball in your glove when beginning your motion. Remember: Always do what feels comfortable to you, but not at the expense of giving the hitter an advantage.

Here is a way to help you grip the ball. First, choose the most difficult grip and position your fingers accordingly while taking the sign from the catcher. If you agree on throwing the pitch for

6

which you've already positioned your fingers, you are all set. If you choose to throw another pitch, one that employs an easier grip, then quickly make the switch with your fingers.

Your front leg is slightly bent, with the front foot (right if you throw right-handed, left if you throw left-handed) extended over the pitching rubber. The toe of the back foot should be touching the back of the rubber. Stand with your feet a bit less than shoulder width apart. Carry your weight on the balls of your feet, with both heels slightly elevated. Some pitchers shift their weight slightly forward in their stance as a reminder to shift it back as they start their motion.

You should have 100 percent confidence in the pitch you're about to throw. If you have any doubt that it's the right pitch for the situation, step off the rubber and and clear your mind.

THE WINDUP

The windup is where most flaws occur in the pitching motion, so it's important to learn the proper fundamentals. To start, take a small step back, shifting your weight back onto the heel of your left foot (right foot if you're left-handed). Just as in hitting, you must go back before you go forward to attain maximum power. Shift the weight of your body forward onto your throwing-side foot so you can push off the rubber with your lower body (see Figure 8).

You still are holding the ball in your pitching hand in the glove. As your weight shifts forward over the rubber, pull your arms into your midsection and then push them down in a

Take a short step back to begin your windup, placing your weight on the back leg (7). As you begin to transfer your weight forward, pull your arms in toward your midsection (8). Next, push your arms down your throwing-side leg as your stride leg begins its move toward the plate (9).

counterclockwise motion. As your glove moves down to the upper thigh on your throwing side, begin to take your stride. The ball remains in the glove.

Extend both arms downward and out in front of you simultaneously, holding the ball in your glove. Break your pitching hand from the glove, raising your arm above your head in a clockwise motion. It should remain fully extended throughout the throwing motion.

THE STRIDE

The stride is probably the most critical step in the pitching motion. The distance, positioning, timing, and plant of the stride are all influential to the direction and velocity of your pitch. The stride is a full-body action. Begin by bending your back forward slightly as your arms push downward and outward. Raise your striding knee up with the glove and extend the knee forward. Extend your arms directly out in front of you while kicking the lower half of your leg. Plant your foot and straighten the leg.

When you stride out, step as far as possible. The farther you stride, the more power you will generate into the pitch. Keep your upper body as tall as possible. The taller you can make yourself, the more power you can get. Allow your leg to slightly bend (see Figure 0-00) when you plant the striding foot. This permits you to transfer your weight over your front side without losing balance. The leg should land on a straight line to home plate. The foot should point to the one-o'clock position (slightly closed). This will allow you to turn your body sideways and add hip rotation to your delivery.

Extend your stride leg out as far as possible during your delivery. This allows you to generate maximum power from your legs and hips.

THE SIDEWAYS ROTATION

Rotating your body sideways as your stride foot lands allows your hips to supplement your throwing motion. As your pitching arm accelerates downward, the hips rotate through with your pitching arm and then square up to the plate. Be careful not to stride off line. It may help you to draw a line in the dirt every time you take the mound. If you open your foot when planting it (pointing toward the catcher), then your hips will open to the plate too early and reduce power from your motion.

PITCHER'S TIP

Sideways rotation is crucial to the pitch for three important reasons:
1. Most women pitchers have hips that are wider than their shoulders. More space is created by turning the body sideways on the stride.
2. The sideways rotation makes the motion more fluid. It is much harder to make a nice, smooth arm circle when you are square to the plate than when you are sideways.
3. By turning your hips sideways and then bringing them around on the follow-through, you involve your hips in the pitching motion, and this will help you generate more power.

— Lisa Fernandez

Your hips and upper body face third base as your lead foot hits the ground. The lead arm (glove arm) first extends toward the target and is then pulled to your chest to help you create a firm front side.

Turning sideways and using your hips will provide you with greater power and more consistent control. This means your front side is facing third base if you are a right-handed pitcher and first base if you're left-handed (see Figure 11). If you do not rotate sideways, you will either hit your hip or you will compensate by moving your arms outward, losing control and power. It is virtually impossible to make a perfect circle with your arm (the ideal) unless you are totally sideways. It takes practice to develop rhythm in rotating your hips through with your arm swing, but the added velocity and control will be well worth the work.

THE FIRM FRONT SIDE

To achieve the optimum stride, your foot must first land with the leg slightly bent. However, as you transfer your weight forward to release the ball, first stiffen that front leg to resist your weight transfer. The front leg provides an axis around which your hips rotate. This helps you attain maximum power—that is, arm speed.

As your weight comes through with the pitch, push up on your front leg to straighten it and make it firm (see Figure 12). Some pitchers even end with a little hop. Finish tall—which means you are keeping the front side firm—rather than finish leaning forward. If the front leg remains bent, there will be very little resistance and your weight will carry out in front of your body. This takes your lower body out of the pitch, causing you to lose power and thus arm speed.

Landing with the lead leg bent (12) enables you to stride out as far as possible. Stiffening the leg (13) creates resistance against your weight shift, adding power to the pitch.

The whole idea of weight transfer and resistance may be difficult for a beginner to comprehend. In fact, some pitchers and coaches at advanced levels do not always understand its importance. A simple method of learning this concept is to pitch standing in front of a tree. Put your foot up against that tree and then go into your motion. If you have a firm front side, you will not hit that tree. If you are not resisting, you'll get a face full of bark.

THE DRAG

When you stride forward with your lead leg, push off the rubber with your throwing side leg, and rotate your forward or planting foot open to help turn your body sideways. As you deliver your pitch, you want your foot on the rubber to follow your motion and drag along the ground. The drag should be on the inside part of the big toe, not on the top of the toe.

Practice this motion without the arm movement because it will help you concentrate on your stride. Practice swinging your striding leg out while pushing off with your other foot and dragging it behind.

The drag continues all the way to the end of the pitch. As the hips begin to open and square up to home plate after the ball is released, dragging your foot becomes a diagonal movement in the direction of the front leg. The foot is finally lifted off the ground, hitting the front leg at about midcalf. Olympic pitcher Lisa Fernandez describes this as "making a figure four."

THE RELEASE

The windup, the stride, the sideways rotation, the firm front side, the drag—all are preparatory movements to getting yourself into good position for the pitching motion's final act—the release.

At the moment your foot lands, your pitching arm should be angled out toward center field with the wrist cocked as if you were showing the ball to the center fielder. Your glove arm should be extended, pointing at the catcher, making sure you are not opening up your hips or shoulders. To an observer in the stands at either foul line, you would appear to be making a giant X with your body (see Figure 26 on page 163).

The arm acts like a whip and should be relaxed throughout the motion. Remember: The windmill pitch is using centrifugal force, so the bigger you can make your arm circle, the more force you are going to create.

During the downswing, extend your arm fully and keep your wrist cocked. Brush your arm right along the front part of your thigh. Keep your palm behind the ball and snap your wrist, releasing the ball right at the hip. As Jay Miller, the head coach at the University of Missouri, says, "You need to have a nice, live wrist," meaning a quick wrist snap and release. A good wrist snap at release will help you keep the ball low. Imagine a book hanging over the edge of a desk. With your hand about six inches underneath the book and facing upward, flip the book off the desk with

The arm should be fully extended, but not tense. Tightness in the arm will slow the arm speed.

—Teresa Wilson, head coach, University of Washington

Your pitching arm must stay relaxed throughout the entire throwing motion. Tension means reduced velocity and control.

14

one swift blow. This is the wrist action you want in your release.

If you snap your wrist hard, the ball will spin in a straight, downward rotation. This helps keep the ball down. Pitches that are low in the strike zone are much more difficult for hitters to handle.

THE FOLLOW-THROUGH

As soon as your arm swing begins its downward motion, square up your hips to home plate. As your arm approaches the release point, open your hips up slightly to allow room for the arm to extend through. (If the hips remained locked, the arm would be forced to come around and/or across your body.) Once the arm gets to the release point, snap your hips around quickly to add power to the pitch. Your hips should be square to home plate (belly button facing the catcher) after the ball is released.

Continue moving your arm in a circle all the way up toward your face, making sure you finish high (see Figure 15). At the very end, and only then, bend at the elbow so it is pointing toward the catcher. You must follow through on every pitch to ensure a good wrist snap, complete extension and maximum velocity. Remember, this is the follow-through for the fastball. Other pitches require a different follow-through.

Always finish your pitches with a strong, high follow-through. The follow-through helps determine location and the amount of spin on the ball.

TERESA WILSON'S EIGHT KEY PITCHING POINTS

1. The pitch is executed in one continuous motion.

2. Make a perfect circle with your arm.

3. The longer the lever, the more force that lever can produce.

4. Pitch on the direct line of force.

5. Open the hips and pitch, then close the hips and follow through.

6. Never guide a pitch. The arm is a noodle.

7 The legs produce the power. The arm produces speed.

8 Power should build throughout the pitch and reach its maximum at the point of release.

In the windmill delivery everything must be performed in a fluid and continuous motion. The pitcher shifts her weight back (18), and then transfers it forward over the rubber. She pulls her arms inward and down in a counter-clockwise motion as she begins to take her stride (19 through 21). As she strides forward, her hands extend outward and separate when they are parallel to the ground. Her pitching hand continues in a backward circle (24) as her body rotates sideways and her weight shifts to the back leg. She lands with a slightly closed front foot and stiffens her lead leg to resist forward movement (26 and 27). As the pitching arm swings through the release point, her hips snap open to face home plate (28 and 29), adding power. After the pitch is released, her back foot drags during the follow-through as her pitching arm finishes high.

PITCHER TRAINING

In general, a pitcher needs to train like any other softball player. She has to participate in flexibility training, weight training, and agility training. However, the pitcher has to be in better shape than anyone else on the field because she is exerting energy on every pitch. Because of this, she must participate in aerobic and anaerobic conditioning as well. In aerobic activity, oxygen is inhaled by the lungs, passed along to the bloodstream, and carried to the working muscles all at a rate that is sufficient to keep up with the muscles' demand for air. Jogging and bicycling are examples of aerobic training. Anaerobic activity is performed at a level that is more intense than the body's oxygen-delivering system can keep up with, such as in sprinting a hundred meters. Section IV covers a basic training program, but there are a few areas in a pitcher's training schedule that are going to differ from those of her teammates.

Pitching is an aerobic activity. You should not be out of breath after you throw a sequence of pitches. However, anaerobic training is helpful because each pitch you throw is a cyclic burst of energy. Sprint workouts are key for this, especially short sprints of about forty yards, performed in rapid succession. Short sprints train your body to exert maximum effort in repetition with short rest times. They train your body to recover quickly, similarly to the way it needs to perform on the pitcher's mound.

BUILDING ENDURANCE

Endurance training is extremely important to pitching and is achieved through aerobic activity. Distance running, jumping rope and other related aerobic exercises help build endurance in your leg muscles and capacity to deliver oxygen to the muscles. Your legs must be strong if you hope to pitch an entire game because the lower half of your body works hard on each pitch. Your legs are the base and the foundation of your pitching mechanics. If your legs tire, your upper body begins to compensate, to substitute a "shortcut" motion or delivery. This can cause problems with your throwing form. When most pitchers begin to tire and lose velocity or control, it's because their legs can no longer maintain proper positioning throughout the delivery. This is why your coach makes you run more than the position players.

Weight training is another area where a pitcher's routine will differ slightly from that of her teammates. Work hard in the off-season to develop strength, but stop lifting weights in preseason. Remember: Your arm should act like a whip and be relaxed throughout the throwing motion. If you work out with heavy weights in-season, your muscles may stiffen and be too tight to whip the ball. Work on form during the season rather than in-

A pitcher needs to develop strong and durable legs. Place a glove beside your right foot. Jump over the glove with both legs and then back again. Continue jumping back and forth for 30 seconds. When time is up, take a rest and repeat the exercise again.

creasing strength. If you feel the need to gain strength during the season, pitch at longer distances so you will build muscle through your pitching motion.

WORKING OUT THE KINKS

All pitchers experience slumps at one time or another. Sometimes pitchers will work extra hard to perfect a certain part of their motion, only to overcompensate and pick up a bad habit somewhere else. The most important thing a pitcher can do when she is going through a slump is to locate the problem as soon as possible. Consult your pitching coach to see if she can detect what the problem is. Another option is to have a coach or a teammate videotape your pitching motion. Seeing your mistakes with your own eyes may provide additional help.

Once you have pinpointed your problem, work on correcting it. For starters, break down the pitching motion step by step. Isolate the area that needs work, and regain the proper feel of that specific motion. If you have trouble extending your stride, rotating sideways, or dragging the back foot, then practice all of these motions without the arm swing or without the release.

If your arm swing is the problem, isolate it by getting down on one knee and throwing the pitch without the rest of your body.

33

Michele Granger delivers a
pitch during the first inning of
the gold medal game in the
1996 Olympics. Granger and
the United States defeated
China, 3–1.

To get the feeling of maximum speed and
relaxation in the arm, the University of
Washington's head coach, Teresa Wilson,
recommends getting into your sideways
rotation and moving the arm in a perfect
circle motion as fast as possible until you
feel a tingly blood rush.

Even the most accomplished pitcher
always look for ways to improve. A favorite drill of the University of Missouri's
head coach, Jay Miller, is the weighted
ball drill, which helps improve speed.
"We weight it two or three ounces from
the normal seven-ounce ball. There are
weighted balls on the market, so you can
buy them or you can make them yourself.
We take one-and-a-half-inch-long finishing nails and pound them into the seam.
About thirty nails equal one ounce.

"Start out every day with a weighted
ball for your warm-up drill. Start at a
short distance and gradually move back
to where you are throwing eighty to a
hundred feet. Then throw long, looping
throws, not line drive types at all, and
work on snapping your wrist and making
the ball spin. That's going to help develop
strength in your wrist and forearm."

TAKING AIM

Move your accuracy drills to a higher
level. Create a target that replicates the strike zone, only smaller.
Draw four corners on your target. See how long it takes you to
reach ten points. If you hit a corner, it is a point. The middle of the
strike zone equals no points, and again, outside the strike zone is
minus one point. See how quickly you can reach ten points, then
twenty points.

Pitching is not like riding a bike. You cannot expect to stop for
an extended period and then simply pick up where you left off.
You need to work at it constantly to maintain your velocity and
accuracy. Not even the cold winters in her native Alaska could
stop Olympic pitcher Michele Granger from practicing. Winters
there were hardly ideal for a softball pitcher's practice, but she
found space in her local church, where she perfected her technique.

Most importantly, make sure you give 100 percent effort when
you are practicing. If you slow your motion to improve your accuracy, you are really not improving at all. As Olympic coach Ralph
Weekly is fond of saying, "Practice does not make perfect. Perfect
practice makes perfect."

DRILL TIME

THE STEP DRILL

Sometimes a pitcher has a problem with her stride; it may not be long enough or forceful enough. To see if that is your problem, have a partner hold a stick in front of you before you begin your motion. As you stride, make sure your foot goes over the stick.

TEN-STRIKE GAME

Working on pitching accuracy can sometimes be boring, so why not turn it into a game? This game can be played with two or more pitchers and a catcher. The object of the game is to throw ten strikes. The first pitcher throws as many balls as it takes to throw ten called strikes. The next pitcher tries to beat that number by throwing fewer pitches to get to ten strikes. The catcher is the judge.

A more advanced game is to count only pitches where the catcher does not have to move her glove to catch the ball. If she moves her glove, it does not count.

Hitting is timing. Pitching is upsetting timing.

34

DEVELOPING YOUR PITCHES

Have you ever hit off of a pitching machine and cranked the speed up really high? At first it seems impossible to catch up to the pitches with your swing. But even a good, hard fastball is not impossible to hit. You just need to adjust—that is, change your approach. You shorten your swing a little, start it a bit sooner, and presto! You

Velocity and control will make you a good pitcher. Movement will make you better.

begin to smack the ball. Good hitters make adjustments according to the pitcher they are facing. It's up to the pitcher to counter those adjustments with an alternate approach.

In the previous chapter you learned that velocity, control, and deception were imperative for achieving pitching success. That still holds true, but at the highest level of softball, the best pitchers mix the speed of their pitches, create movement on them, and lure hitters to swing at pitches out of the strike zone. To have success at advanced levels, you need to learn how to make the ball drop, rise, curve, knuckle, and tail away from the hitter. Most importantly, you need to vary the speed of your pitches. Challenging hitters with fastballs on the edges of the strike zone will no longer be enough to remain successful. You will need to learn how to keep batters off balance and guessing at your next pitch. This especially helps pitchers who don't have great velocity. Being able to change speed makes their fastball look faster. Hitters continually improve their game. To remain one step ahead, you need to do the same.

MASTER THE BASICS

Lisa Fernandez did not throw advanced pitches the first time she stood atop a pitcher's mound. She took many years to learn the proper fundamentals, then she steadily mastered different pitches through trial and error. You should take the same approach. Before moving on to advanced pitching, you must perfect your pitching mechanics, you must master striding, rotating, resisting, and getting a good leg drive. Age is not a factor. Even a ten-year-old who has smooth mechanics and can consistently locate her fastball is ready to add to her pitching repertoire. On the other hand, a high-school pitcher who still struggles with the basics is not.

CHANGE-UP

The change-up is the first advanced pitch that a pitcher should add to her arsenal. The change-up (also called the off-speed pitch) is a pitch slower than the fastball; it throws off a batter's timing. The hitter has only about two-tenths of a second to decide whether she should swing. Within those two-tenths of a second, the batter has to detect whether the pitch is high or low, inside or outside, and if the spin on the pitch will influence the ball enough to curve, tail, drive, or rise in or out of the strike zone. A change in speeds adds another factor the hitter must consider. Too many factors and too little time give the pitcher an advantage.

You can create an off-speed pitch in a number of different ways. Try experimenting to see which method works best for you. The most effective change-up appears to the batter to be a fastball out of the pitcher's hand—a pitch thrown with the same motion and spin on the ball as the fastball. If the hitter thinks the pitch is a fastball, she'll swing too early, causing her to miss the pitch, hit it weakly, or pull it foul. In addition, when you can consistently throw your change-up for strikes, you'll be surprised at your ability to sneak your fastball by hitters. A good change-up keeps the hitter off-balance.

When you are first learning to throw a change-up, keep it simple. You can make minor alterations. The simplest variation? Tighten your grip on the ball. Keep your fingers in the same position as you would when throwing a fastball, but squeeze the ball tightly with your fingers. Holding the ball extra tight like this will decrease your velocity (see Chapter 8), which is the primary goal when throwing a change-up. Another slight change is to grip the ball back in your palm. Instead of holding the ball out in the fingers, jam it back in your hand. You diminish the velocity of your pitch by decreasing the snap during the delivery.

Both of these changes will not cause a major reduction in speed when compared to your fastball, but enough to disrupt the

Speed is not necessarily everything. Christa Williams, probably the hardest thrower in the game, gets up to about sixty-nine miles per hour, but there are many top pitchers who cannot come close to that, yet who win consistently. Movement is more important than speed. Movement keeps the hitter off-balance.

—Lisa Fernandez, pitcher, U.S. Olympic team

The game used to be so pitcher-dominated. But now there is the new bat technology, a livelier, red-seamed ball, and they have moved the pitchers back.

—John Rittman, head coach, Stanford University

2

Hold the ball tightly in the back of your hand to reduce the velocity of your fastball.

hitter's timing (about six to eight miles per hour difference). They are easy to learn and have the same pitching motion as the fastball. Deception is the key to a good change-up.

Change-ups are very effective against hitters who frequently pull the ball. They are more likely to open their hips and shoulders too early, as if they were expecting a fastball. Another good time to throw a change-up is when you've thrown a bunch of fastballs consecutively to the batter. Just when the hitter will think she has the fastball timed, you toss her the change-up and watch her get fooled.

There are several other types of change-ups. The knuckleball can also be used as a change-up. Some have different grips, while others have different throwing motions. The most common are the circle change-up, the backhand change-up, and the stiff-wrist change-up. Experiment with each type of off-speed pitch to find one you're comfortable throwing. You may even want to carry more than one change-up in your bag of tricks. But make sure it's an effective pitch before you use it in a game. The best test is to mix it in when throwing to a batter. If the hitter is fooled by the pitch (early with her swing), it is effective. If she's taking good swings and hitting the ball hard, it's not ready for competition.

THE CIRCLE CHANGE

The circle change is the most popular. And it is easy to control. Lay your pinkie finger alongside and thumb underneath the ball. Place the three middle fingers on top of the ball. Put pressure on the ball with your thumb (underneath) and middle finger (on top) while the others lay limp on the ball. You are essentially trying to make a circle with the thumb and middle or ring finger around the ball. This will automatically push the ball a little farther back into your palm, making it impossible to throw it as hard as the fastball. As a result, you can still have the same wrist snap you use in your fastball motion, which gives the ball the identical spin. Follow through to about chest level.

THE BACKHANDED CHANGE

The backhanded change-up is a deceptive pitch, too, because the grip and the motion look very similar to those used for the fastball. The difference comes at the point of release. Take the same grip you would for the fastball. As your arm circles downward to the release point, keep your hand on top of the ball so the ball is facing the ground. Do not turn your hand over to get underneath the ball. As you release the ball, face the back of your hand toward the catcher and flip the ball out of your hand. This is why it is called a backhanded change-up. Keep your wrist snap below the waist. If the wrist goes above the waist, the ball will travel too high, out of the strike zone. (A firm snap gives the ball the look and feel of a fastball.)

This pitch is effective only when the pitcher puts applies maximum effort in the hand and arm action. Without a firm wrist snap, the ball won't reach home plate. The intensity of the pitcher's motion coaxes the hitter into preparing for a fastball, yet the pitch comes in much slower. The drawback is that an observant hitter may recognize the difference in release and realize that an off-speed pitch is coming.

The arm speed of the backhanded change-up deceives hitters into believing they're looking at a fastball. The change-up pitch is key because hitting is timing, and the change-up ruins a batter's timing.

THE STIFF-WRIST CHANGE

The stiff-wrist change is another effective change-up, and it's easy to learn. Keep your motion and your grip the same as you use for the fastball. When you release the ball, however, keep your wrist stiff. In other words, lock your wrist so it does not snap after you release the ball. This stops the ball from spinning, and the lack of snap will slow down the ball considerably. However, the absence of spin can alert astute hitters that the pitch is a change-up.

THE KNUCKLEBALL

For the knuckleball, grip the ball so your knuckles are behind the ball. Usually you use two or three fingers in this manner. With the seams making a C facing you, dig your fingertips under the top seams. Grip the sides of the ball with your thumb and pinkie finger.

Lisa Fernandez is one of the all-time great softball players. You'll find her either at third base or on the pitcher's mound, setting records in every category. She can hit and field like a superstar, but her pitching accomplishments are legendary. Here is a summary of what Lisa has achieved on the softball field.

In College (University of California, Los Angeles)

- Led UCLA to two NCAA championships and two second-place finishes in four years
- 93–7 pitching record, an all-time NCAA high
- Forty-two consecutive wins
- Pitched ninety-seven consecutive shutout innings
- Career ERA of 0.22
- Senior year, led the nation in **both** ERA (0.25) and batting average (.510)
- Four-time All-American
- Three-time Honda Award winner
- First softball player ever to win the Honda-Broderick Award, given to the top female athlete in college sports

In the Olympics

- Member of the 1996 gold-medal-winning team
- Pitched twenty-two innings, more than any other U.S. player
- Allowed only four hits
- ERA of 0.33
- Struck out thirty-two batters
- Saved the gold-medal game by striking out three of the four batters she faced
- Recorded the first RBI of the Olympics with a single that scored Dot Richardson

And a Few More Amazing Facts

- Seven-time gold-medal winner in international competition
- Four-time Amateur Softball Association All-American
- ASA Sportswoman of the Year, 1991 and 1992

The change-up is one of the most devastating pitches. Just about any hitter in the game would rather face a pitcher who throws really hard than one who might throw not quite as hard but also has a change.

—Lisa Fernandez

The delivery is exactly the same as for the stiff-wrist change-up—use the same motion as for your fastball, but lock your wrist upon release. Your arm should be locked at the elbow. As you let go of the ball, push outward with the fingers you had dug under the seam. There should be very little or no rotation on the ball.

The most difficult aspect of throwing the knuckleball with success is timing your release. You have to release while you are pushing the ball. If you release too early or too late, you will lose control of the ball's flight. The only way to find your release point for the knuckleball is to practice throwing it over and over again. Eventually you will become familiar with the right point of release.

THE RISE

The rise pitch breaks upward. Its spin is a backward or upward spin. Because the air resistance is greater underneath the ball, the force from the resistance pushes the ball up. The pitch will not rise as much as a drop pitch drops because it is working against gravity. Release the ball to maximum rotation on the ball. Without this spin, the ball will not rise.

The rise pitch can be especially devastating to hitters. When a pitch appears as if it's going to be a strike, a hitter's eyes are trained to send a message to the brain that tells the body to swing. Any pitch that drops, curves, or tails out of strike zone makes it difficult for the hitter to make contact. But when the ball rises out of the strike zone, it is nearly impossible to make contact. When hitters start their swing, their first movement is to bring the hands and bat down. If the pitch drops down or curves away, they have a chance to adjust by dropping the barrel of the bat or extending out or pulling in their arms. There is no chance for a hitter to raise her swing once she has made the initial move downward. You simply cannot adjust your swing upward in time "to catch up with the pitch." The best she can do is foul the pitch off or pop it up.

Place the index finger and the ring finger across two wide seams as the main grippers; lay the middle finger flat in the middle. Place the pinkie and the thumb on the ball's sides as guides. Don't grip the ball tightly. Make sure the ball is in the pads of your fingers and not your palm.

Another rise ball grip that advanced pitchers use requires strength in the pitching forearm. Take the two seams closest together and place the ring finger and middle finger slightly to the left of the seams. Curl the index finger slightly, similar to the knuckleball grip. When you curl it, the pressure will be on the inside part of the tip of that index finger. This grip is very difficult to master initially because of the pressure of the grip, but it gives you the maximum amount of movement.

The best change-ups have a lot of spin versus those that spin very little. One reason I do not teach the knuckleball very much is that good hitters look for spin first thing and if you see no spin, then it is a dead giveaway.

—Teresa Wilson, head coach, University of Washington

Using a pitch that is changing planes as it approaches the hitter is one of the most effective ways to create ground balls, fly balls, and strikeouts. As coaches, we teach our hitters to stay balanced. Having a rise ball will keep opponents' hitters off-balance.

—Roanna Brazier, head coach, University of Ohio

To throw the rise pitch, hold the ball in the pads of your fingers (4). As you release the pitch, roll the ball off your hand. Your index finger is the last part of your hand to touch the ball. (5) illustrates the proper follow-through for a rise pitch.

You really have to resist in order to get under that ball. I try to stride slightly across my midline because that helps me block my hip from coming around. I'm still going to square up, but I want to lag that hip slightly so I can let my wrist snap.

—Lisa Fernandez

When throwing the rise pitch, lead with the inside part of your elbow on the downswing. (Your pitching hand should slightly trail your elbow.) As you approach the release point, your palm should point toward third base (first base for a left-hander), and your fingers should sit underneath the ball. When you release the ball, you want to cut underneath the ball with your hand. Your palm faces the sky as the ball rolls off your hand. The ball should last touch your index finger when it leaves your hand. This motion (cutting underneath the ball) gives the ball its backward rotation. Your follow-through goes straight up and finishes high.

Keep your body low to the ground. Because the ball is rising, you want your release point to be as low as possible. Take a long stride and keep the back leg bent to stay low to the ground. It might help to think about trying to scrape your fingers along the ground. Pitchers have a tendency to short-arm the rise pitch to get underneath the ball better, but you want to keep your arm as long as possible and still avoid contacting the ground.

A good drill for the rise ball is to get about sixty feet away from the catcher. The extra distance will allow you to see the flight of the ball. It is instant feedback, because sometimes it is hard to pick up rotation and flight at the normal distance. With the extra space, you can really analyze your pitch. If you are throwing it high, it is because you are arching your back or short-arming it. When the ball is curving too much you are not getting fully underneath the ball for the up snap. If it is rising too soon, you need to release the ball a little earlier.

DROP BALL

The drop ball breaks downward. It's popular because it induces batters to hit ground balls. You want the drop ball to accelerate its break about four feet out from home plate. There are two methods of getting your pitch to drop. They are called the peel drop and the turnover drop. Both drop pitches are very tough on hitters who swing with an uppercut.

THE PEEL DROP

The peel drop is very similar to a fastball. You use the same grip and the same motion as for your fastball. It is called the peel drop because you peel your fingers off the ball. For this pitch you want to shorten your stride and push your upper body slightly over the stride foot. This enables the weight of your body to get over the top of the ball, producing an earlier release. Make sure you don't shorten your stride too much. Olympic pitcher Lisa Fernandez estimates that her fastball stride is about eight feet long, and her drop ball stride is about six inches shorter. To remain deceptive, there cannot be a big difference in your stride.

To make the ball drop, get your palm on top of the ball. The release point is a bit sooner (more toward your back leg) than for the fastball. Just before you release the ball, your fingers are pointing down to the ground. As you release, pull up on the ball and snap your wrist. Your fingers should make a fist after the ball is thrown.

Your shoulders dictate what the location of the pitch will be. They should finish square to home plate on a pitch down the middle. If you want to go inside to a right-handed hitter, keep your

---

TURNOVER VS. PEEL

Lisa Fernandez, Olympic pitcher

When you throw the peel drop you'll get more speed, and when you throw the rollover drop, you'll get more movement, which I think is more important. In my mind, deception and movement are the keys to a successful pitcher. It might be easier for pitchers to learn the peel drop, but eventually they should learn the rollover.

Teresa Wilson, head coach, University of Washington

If I have an option of teaching the drop to a pitcher, I'd use the peel drop. Most pitchers are known for one pitch. They grow up either throwing the rise or throwing the drop, and they limit themselves. But rarely do they throw both pitches well. I teach the peel drop because the release is then the same for the rise and the drop and the screwball or curveball, basically only with a quarter-turn variation on your wrist. If young pitchers are taught that way, it allows them to throw more pitches off the same basic set of mechanics. Then we'd have more pitchers who could throw a wider variety of pitches.

This is the grip for the turnover drop pitch. Your hand remains on top of the ball as you release the pitch.

On any pitch you are learning, the only thing that's important is the rotation on the ball. How you hold it and how you throw it really are irrelevant if you can get that ball to spin. That's going to determine whether the ball is going to break. When you are teaching any pitch, the thing you want to work on is getting the right rotation of the ball.

—Jay Miller, head coach, University of Missouri

shoulders more open. To throw outside to a righty, rotate your shoulders more.

THE TURNOVER DROP

The turnover (or rollover) drop requires a distinct grip and delivery. Place your fingers to the side. A right-handed pitcher holds her three middle fingers on the right side of the ball; a left-handed pitcher grips the ball to the left. Instead of your fingers covering that "C" formed by the seams, the seams are now visible. As your arm completes its downward swing, the throwing shoulder lifts up slightly. (Picture your shoulder blade raising up, as if you were shrugging your shoulders.) This allows your hand to get over the top of the ball. As you release the ball, turn your hand over so the palm faces the ground, and then drive the ball downward. This gives the ball forward rotation (topspin), which makes the ball drop. When you have completed your follow-through, your fingers should point down at the ground.

The drop pitch forces hitters to hit the ball on the ground, so it is an especially valuable pitch when you need an infield ground ball out to get you out of a jam. A great drill for practice is to set up a string that runs across the front of home plate (you could use two sticks on each side of the plate). Run it about four feet in front of the plate at about knee level. The goal is to throw your drop pitch so it goes over the string but hits the plate.

CURVEBALL

The key to throwing a curveball is the extended follow-through. Hold the ball as if you were going to throw a two-seam fastball. Push the index and middle fingers together. As you deliver the pitch, keep your hand underneath the ball, with the palm facing up. Turn you hand over the top of the ball as you release. The motion should be the same as if you were turning a doorknob. This gives the ball a sideways (or horizontal) spin as it travels to the plate. Pull your arm across your body on the follow-through.

Use the curveball wisely. Do not locate the ball so it curves across the middle of the plate. Start it down the middle so it

CHAPTER 9

Hold the index and middle fingers together when throwing a curveball (7). As you release the pitch, cut across your body with your pitching arm to produce a sideways spin on the ball (8).

curves to the corner of the plate when throwing a pitch for a strike. If you are ahead in the count and are trying to make the hitter swing at a bad pitch, start your curveball on the corner so it curves out of the strike zone. The curveball is extremely tough on batters who hit from the same side as you throw (e.g., right-handed hitter vs. right-handed pitcher).

Blending Two Pitches

There may be times when you combine the mechanics of two pitches to create a new pitch for your repertoire. As long as you are comfortable throwing the pitch, try it out on hitters in practice. If the pitch is effective, give it a shot in the game.

One example of this would be a drop-curveball. This is a common pitch thrown at the college level. Take the grip and release from the turnover drop, add the follow-through of the curveball and you're now throwing a drop-curveball. This pitch has downward movement because of the top spin, but by pulling your arm across your body on the follow through, it will also have sideways movement.

A screwball is a cross between a fastball and a rise pitch. Grip the ball as if you were throwing a two-seam fastball. Put pressure on your index finger and deliver the pitch with the same arm motion as you would for the fastball. As you release, cut underneath the ball (as you would when throwing a rise pitch) to give it 7 to 1 o'clock rotation if you're right-handed—5 to 11 o'clock if you're

Here is the proper technique for throwing a drop-curveball. The motion is identical to a fastball up until the release point (10). When you release the pitch, turn your hand over the ball so your palm faces the ground, and drive your arm downward and across your body. This movement creates a 10 o'clock to 4 o'clock spin that makes the pitch curve down and across the plate.

left-handed. Do not cut underneath the ball quite as much as the rise pitch, but enough to spin the ball so it tails (breaks slightly to the side of your pitching arm). A right-handed screwball will tail in on a right-handed batter and away from a left-handed batter.

DRILL TIME

THE SNAP DRILL

When you make advanced pitches, most of your motion remains the same. The things that change the most are your grip and your snap, so it helps to isolate these when you are learning. Stand sideways, as if you have already taken your stride, about ten feet from a partner. Throw your pitch without the windup and with just a slight backswing, working on getting most of your power from your wrist snap. Work on all the pitches this way until you feel comfortable with the different releases.

CALLING YOUR PITCHES

The ability to create movement on your pitches is helpful, but you must be able to throw these pitches to each part of the strike zone. In this drill, you will tell the hitter you're facing what pitch you're throwing. You need your catcher and a few hitters. Throw to the hitters as if it were a real game having the catcher call balls and strikes. The difference, though, is that you are only allowed to throw one type of pitch during the at-bat and you must tell the batter what pitch it is you're throwing. For example, for the first round of hitters, you will only throw your drop pitch. The batters will be aware that every incoming pitch will be a drop pitch. This forces you to concentrate on throwing to different locations of the strike zone. Because you cannot fool the hitter, you will have to throw her inside, outside, high, and low. For the second round, pick a different pitch.

12

Add as many pitches to your arsenal as you can. Fooling the batter is a beautiful thing.

ADVANCED PITCHING

I n school there are two ways to prepare for your class exams. You can either study the material thoroughly and thus enter the test with confidence, or you can arrive unprepared and hope you will be given questions with which you're familiar. It's a safe bet that ninety-nine times out of a hundred, your results will be better when you prepare thoroughly for the examination. Pitching preparation is no different. You must prepare thoroughly.

The difference between good pitchers and great ones is how well they think.

PREGAME PREPARATION

Pitching requires both physical and mental preparation. Game preparation begins when you arrive at the field. Your thoughts and actions should be focused on getting yourself ready for the game. Begin stretching your muscles; get them loose and limber. Stretching increases flexibility. With a pitching motion like the windmill delivery, flexibility is critical to a safe, injury-free delivery. If you haven't stretched properly, you're risking injury. Stretching exercises are covered in Section IV.

Once you are stretched out, have a catch with a teammate throwing overhand. The pitcher becomes an infielder once the pitch is delivered and will have to make overhand throws during the game. Make sure your arm is loose throwing overhand.

Loosen your arm by throwing the ball overhand (2). Later, work on proper pitching mechanics and establish confidence in each pitch you plan to throw during the game (3).

About twenty minutes before game time, warm up with a catcher in the bullpen. Stand about three-quarters of the distance from the mound to home plate (thirty feet) and toss the ball underhand with ease to the catcher. Do not go into your full pitching motion at this point. Just gradually loosen your arm and lower body. Continue this until you feel that your arms and legs are loose. Next, work on the spins of your pitches. Throw each about fifteen to twenty times or until you feel comfortable getting the proper spin with accuracy.

After you've practiced the grips and the spins of all your pitches, you are ready to throw from full distance. Using your entire windup and pitching motion, throw each pitch about ten times. At this point you may realize that one or two of your pitches are not working for you. If you don't feel comfortable throwing them in the bullpen, you probably won't want to throw them in the game, at least not right away.

Finish throwing about five minutes before the game starts. This will give you enough time to rest and review with your teammates the opposing team's lineup. Make sure you have a jacket to wear in the dugout between innings. The jacket will help keep your arm warm and loose.

Pitchers should grow up as total athletes. I want them to pitch, but I also want them to hit, to field, to run bases.

— Teresa Wilson, head coach, University of Washington

VISUALIZATION

Stretching and throwing pitches in the bullpen get the body loose before game time, but how do you stimulate the brain to get the mind working? Visualization is a very simple process. You train your brain to think positive thoughts. This can be practiced during the ride to the game, sitting in the dugout, or getting a drink of water.

Many athletes like to play the game in their imagination before it starts. It puts them in a positive frame of mind, which helps give them confidence entering the game. If you are scheduled to pitch, visualize yourself throwing all your pitches for strikes. Imagine throwing your drop pitch and hitters swinging over the top of the ball. Think about a hitter taking a knee-high fastball for a called third strike. Visualization is not only simple, it can be fun, too.

Visualization can also help when you have the pregame jitters. If you are fighting nerves, close your eyes and place yourself in a pleasant atmosphere. Imagine a peaceful lake, a sparkling waterfall, or sitting on the beach near the ocean. To relax your body, you must first put your mind at ease.

PITCHING STRATEGY

At some point in your pitching career you may have heard your head coach or pitching coach tell you, "Each pitch should have a purpose." What this means is that each time you deliver a ball to the plate, have an idea in mind (or a purpose) of what you want that particular pitch to accomplish. It may be to get ahead in the count (more strikes than balls), to set up the hitter for the next pitch, to expose a hitter's weakness, or to get her to chase a pitch

Think location when you're facing a slap hitter. Try to hit the corner. Anything away from the middle of the plate is a hard pitch for the slap hitter to handle.

out of the strike zone. Whatever the case may be, you should never throw a pitch without thinking about its purpose.

The best approach for young pitchers is to make the first pitch a strike. To record outs, you need to throw strikes. It is important to work ahead in the count. If the count is in your favor, then you can work on throwing to the edges of the strike zone. The batter will have a much tougher time hitting pitches on the corners. If you're behind in the count (more balls than strikes), the hitter can wait for a pitch down the middle of the strike zone.

Throwing a quick strike also decreases your chances of walking the batter. Bases on balls are devastating to pitchers. Not only does the hitter reach first base, but also you allow her to do so without earning it. This can affect you psychologically. Working ahead in the count takes the pressure off yourself and allows you to focus on making good pitches.

SETTING UP THE HITTER

Advanced pitchers often throw pitches to set up hitters. Setting up a hitter simply means throwing a pitch that will set her up to be fooled on the next pitch. Here is how that works. Suppose your first pitch to the batter is a fastball called for a strike on the outside corner. The next pitch thrown is a change-up on the inside corner that the hitter pulls foul. With the count at no balls and two strikes, you are way ahead of the hitter. Take note that the batter has seen one pitch that was thrown hard and outside, and an off-speed pitch that was thrown inside. The next pitch you throw is a hard fastball that is high and inside for a ball. This is called a purpose pitch. It was not thrown for the hitter to swing at, but to set her up for the next pitch. Throwing that pitch plants a seed in the batter's mind that she has to start her swing early and be quick with the bat if she's going to make contact with a hard fastball on the inside corner. Your next pitch, however, is an off-speed pitch on the outside corner. The hitter (in most cases) will be very early with her swing and either miss it or hit it weakly.

Another approach to setting up the hitter is to throw pitches on the outside corner early in the count. Most hitters do not like outside pitches and won't swing at them unless they have two strikes. Get ahead in the count by throwing strikes on the outside corner. Many batters will then lean out over the plate and look for a pitch outside. Now you throw a hard pitch on the inside corner. This will most likely freeze the hitter, who will look at a third strike, or she'll swing late and hit the ball weakly below the barrel of the bat (get jammed).

DEFINING THE ROLE OF YOUR PITCHES

Once you are able to throw a variety of pitches (fastball, drop, rise, etc.), you should define the role of each pitch. In specific

game situations you may need a strike-out, a ground ball, a pop fly, or a pitch on the outside corner. Get comfortable with each pitch's craft. For example, many pitches rely on their fastball when they have to throw a strike. Some pitchers may throw a rise pitch when they need the batter to swing and miss. A number of pitchers throw a drop pitch when they're hoping for a ground ball. Part of perfecting your pitching repertoire is understanding how each pitch works best for you.

Among your menu of pitches you will develop a "best pitch." This is the pitch you go to when the game is on the line. If you throw a blazing fastball, your fastball may be your best pitch. Maybe your change-up is so deceptive that it becomes your top pitch. In any event, your best pitch is what you should rely on in a tight situation. You never want to get beaten by the hitter and then say to yourself, "Why didn't I throw her my best pitch?" Never get beaten with anything less than your best.

With all of this said, do not fall into predictable pitch patterns. Vary your pitch patterns throughout the game. Remember: Deception is as important as movement and velocity. Keep the hitters guessing by mixing your pitches with intelligence.

Michele Smith won two games during the 1996 Olympics, allowing just three runs on eight hits in 14 innings, while striking out 23 batters.

SCOUTING YOUR OPPONENTS

The best way to defeat your opponents is to get to know them as well as you can. All hitters have strengths and weaknesses. Good pitchers stay away from hitters' strengths and attack their weaknesses. To determine how to combat your opponents, you must be very observant and watchful each time you have an opportunity to see them hit.

At the college level, you may face teams many times and possess scouting reports on hitters. In that case you enter the game with some idea of their strengths and weaknesses. If you are playing a team for the first time, you will need to learn as you go, but there are a few opportunities to see hitters swing before you face them.

Watch pregame batting practice if possible. Take note of each hitter and look for obvious strengths and weaknesses. Do they

Stay away from the middle of the plate when facing good hitters. Even the best batters struggle against pitchers who can "paint the black."

seem to like pitches inside or outside? How do they handle low pitches and high pitches? Are they free swingers (swing at nearly everything), or do they swing at only strikes? Is their swing long, or is it short? Hitters with long swings are more susceptible to fast pitches. Do they practice slap hits or drag bunts?

If a team does not take batting practice before the game, take a quick look at their practice swings when they're on deck or before they step into the batter's box. Check the arc of their swing. Is it level, an uppercut, or a slightly downward (chopping) swing? This bit of information may help dictate your pitch selection. Some hitters give away weaknesses by their stance or by where they stand in the box. For example, a hitter who holds her hands low will almost always have trouble with high strikes. If they stand far away from the plate, they probably like to get their arms extended, so you may want to pitch them inside.

The best information available is what a hitter does when she faces you. Obviously, this can't be executed into your game plan until the later innings, but it can be very helpful. If you've gotten the hitter out, pay attention to how you got her out. Did she swing at pitches out of the strike zone? Was she late on your fastball? Does she have trouble keeping her weight back on off-speed pitches on the outside part of the plate? Acknowledge the pitches you threw to get her out and their location.

On the other hand, if a batter has been crushing your pitches early in the game, store that information as well. If you tried to come inside with a fastball and she smacked it for a double, stay away from throwing hard pitches inside. If she's been hitting rise pitches up in the strike zone, try countering with a drop pitch low in the strike zone. Good pitchers make adjustments as the game progresses.

To really execute a successful pitching plan, you need to forge a close relationship with your catcher. This pitcher/catcher combination is often referred to as "the battery," and like another battery, the two ends need to work together to get power flowing smoothly between them. Pitchers and catchers need to make that connection for a number of reasons. Your catcher will have a very good idea of what pitches are working best for you that day. If your curveball is flat (not breaking sharply), she's got the best view and knows not to call for that pitch. The catcher may also recognize weaknesses in the batter. This allows the pitcher to simply concentrate on throwing her pitches while the catcher focuses on setting up the hitter and attacking her weaknesses. When the pitcher and catcher are comfortable working together, it is a big advantage to the team.

Make sure you're on the same page with your catcher for every pitch. Here, U.S. Olympic team catcher Gillian Boxx talks things over with teammate Lisa Fernandez.

I think a good catcher can make a good pitcher great, and I think an average catcher can really hurt a pitcher.
—Cindy Cohen, head coach, Princeton University

TEN TIPS FOR THE PITCHER

❶ Look at the batter's position in the box. If she is way back in the box, she probably does not have a very quick swing and is trying to give herself more time. Look to throw your fastball. If your fastball lacks velocity, try the drop pitch The drop will practically be in the dirt when it reaches her, yet it will have been a strike when it crossed the plate.

❷ If a hitter stands in the front of the box, go with your fastball inside. She will have less time to react. The rise ball is a good one for this type of hitter, too. Start it out low so it rises into the strike zone as it passes her.

❸ Pitch the hitter inside if she's using a closed stance. She'll have trouble getting her hips open in time to get the barrel of the bat on the ball.

8

4 Pitch the hitter outside if she has an open stance.

5 Pitch a slap hitter inside. It will slow down her momentum to first base, and it's a tough pitch for her to handle. Most slappers try to hit the ball by the shortstop, so they look for an outside pitch. Keep the pitch inside and low in the strike zone.

6 In a bunt situation, throw high strikes. It may force a pop-up.

7 Throw a change-up to a hitter who has just pulled a fastball foul. If she is in front of your fastball, she'll be way out in front of a change-up.

8 If the batter is a power hitter, pitches low and away are your best bet. She will not be able to get maximum strength into her swing.

9 If the player has a reputation to swing at everything, stay away from the strike zone. Why throw her a good pitch when she'll swing at one out of the strike zone?

10 Always stay ahead in the count. In that way you'll force the batter to hit your best pitch. If you fall behind, the hitter gains the advantage.

This is smart pitching. The batter took a stance well off the plate, exposing herself to outside strikes. The pitcher hit her spot and the result was a weak ground ball back to the mound.

SCOUTING DRILL

One of our favorite pitching exercises is to take our next opponents and set up innings using their hitters. If we know the team, the way we know the entire PAC-10, after their warm-ups, our pitchers start throwing innings to "the other team." Instead of just saying this batter is a lefty or this batter is a righty, we will put a name to them so we get practice pitching around each batter's strengths and going for her weaknesses, whether she has speed or not, so we create the game. By the time we play them that week, we have already played them a few times in our mind and in our practice. And it is fun. They keep the count, and if they throw a fat pitch, they say that the batter got a single or a double or hit it out if it is a great hitter.

— Teresa Wilson

ADJUSTING TO GAME SITUATIONS

An exciting aspect of pitching is that no game is ever the same. Each time you take the mound, there is a different condition that requires you to adjust your approach. Hitters vary, the weather conditions often have an effect on the hitters, pitchers, and fielders, and your personal talents often change from game to game. On some days you may not be able to control your rise pitch. On other days you have a little extra zip on your fastball. Factoring in the different elements each game adds flavor to the thrill of competition.

THE UMPIRE'S STRIKE ZONE

The person who has the authority to influence your performance more than anyone in uniform is the umpire behind the plate. No matter how well scouted a team might be or how versatile your pitching is, the home plate ump can heavily influence your pitching performance and ultimately the outcome of the game. Just as you need to get a feel for your pitches and the hitters you're facing in the early innings, you must learn the umpire's strike zone immediately.

Umpires are notorious for having their own interpretation of the strike zone. The best advice to follow is to discover what it is and to adjust your pitches accordingly. Do not get upset over called balls and strikes, and do not argue about the umpire's judgment. It takes away your focus on the job at hand, and quite frankly, it will not help. If the umpire is not calling pitches strikes

that you feel are in the strike zone, yelling at her won't change her mind. It may even work against you and your teammates.

Most umpires differ with the vertical strike zone. Some umps call low strikes and not high ones, while others do the exact opposite. Pay attention to her pattern and use it to your advantage. The width of the strike zone is fairly consistent among umpires. You will run into some who have a narrow strike zone and others who have a wide strike zone. If you notice that the ump is calling pitches off the plate a strike, by all means use that to your advantage as well.

Take advantage of any situation that allows you to pitch out of the strike zone. For example, if the umpire is consistently calling high pitches as strikes, pitch to that location. Also, if a hitter has been chasing low balls all day, feed her more low balls.

INNING, OUTS, AND SCORE

Getting outs is a simple way to phrase the pitcher's mission. How you go about getting them changes through the course of the game. The inning, score, and number of outs may influence how you pitch to a hitter.

A lot of times you'll hear coaches say, "Just throw strikes." This advice cannot always be applied to the situation at hand. For example, say it's a tie score and there is a runner on third base with two outs late in the game. The opposing team's best   hitter is at the plate. It doesn't make sense to throw her strikes because there is nobody occupying first base. Pitch around her (don't throw her any good pitches) and try to get her to chase a bad pitch. If she swings, you're out of a jam. If she walks, then you've gotten past their best hitter without giving up any runs.

Before you toe the rubber, remind yourself that you're a fielder, too. Know exactly what you're going to do with the ball if it's hit to you.

Another situation that may dictate your pitches is if there is a runner on third with fewer than two outs. A fly ball to the outfield will score the runner, so you want her to hit the ball on the ground. A steady diet of low strikes and drop pitches is all the batter should see in this situation. High strikes are easy to hit in the air.

A mistake pitchers frequently make is changing their pitching strategy when their team gets a big lead. Pitchers often think they should just throw the ball over the plate to make hitters swing the bat to record outs. This is the wrong approach to take. Your team is winning, so why do anything differently? Stick with what has worked for you up to that point. Continue to pitch as if the score were 0–0.

FIELDING YOUR POSITION

Before the softball is on its flight to the plate, the defense consists of a pitcher, a catcher, and seven players in the field. Once the ball is released by the pitcher, there are eight players in the field. Part of the pitcher's responsibility is to learn to field her position. With the popularity of bunting and slap hitting in women's fast-pitch softball, a pitcher's defensive skills are critical.

To field your position adequately, you must develop quick reactions. You are standing fewer than forty-three feet from home plate, so the ball gets to you in a hurry. After your follow-through is completed, prepare yourself for a ball hit back to the mound.

The best time to work on your quickness and agility off the mound is in practice. Throw pitches at full speed, and have a coach or teammate hit ground balls at you as you're releasing the ball. As you improve at this drill, have them hit balls to your left and right to increase your range. Working hard at your fielding will only help your pitching success.

How much you are able to contribute to bunt coverages is significant to your team's defense. If you can cover the territory in front of you, it takes a lot of pressure off of the first and third basemen. At times you may tell the third baseman to stay put and you'll cover all balls to your right. This would be valuable in a situation where there were no outs and runners on first and second bases. The third baseman can stay on the bag for the force-out while you field the bunt.

The less area the first and third basemen feel responsible to cover, the farther back they can set up in the ready position. Their range improves immediately, which tightens up the entire defense. A hard-hit ball that gets by them playing fifteen feet in front of the base quickly turns into a routine groundout when they're positioned four feet in front of the base. Work hard in practice at running in to field balls and also moving from side to side.

Because you have very little time to react to the ball as it comes off the bat, it is extremely important to know where you are going to throw the ball before you deliver the pitch. Make sure you ask yourself where you're going to throw in specific situations. For example, with a runner on first base, if a ball is hit right back to you, the throw goes to second base to get the force-out. If the batter bunts toward the third-base line and you field it, the throw goes to first base. Any hesitation on your part may   allow the runners to be safe all around.

BACKING UP BASES

On balls that are not hit in your vicinity, you need to think about backing up one of the bases. At various times you will be called on to back up first, third, and home plate on throws. In these situations, you need to be about fifteen feet behind the base and in line with the throw. If the ball gets past the baseman or catcher, you are there to field the ball and stop any baserunners from advancing. If you are not in position backing up, it can be very costly to the team.

There are several other instances where the pitcher's presence is needed in the infield. When a baserunner is caught between bases, you need to get involved in the rundown. On a ball hit to the right side of the infield that takes the first baseman away from first base, you may have to cover the open base. Also on a wild-pitch or passed-ball situation with a runner on third base, you must cover home plate to take the throw.

Because pitchers have the extra responsibility of developing

Don't become a spectator on the mound. Back up bases, help out on rundowns, and do whatever else it takes to help your team get an out.

Don't protect your pitchers. Our pitchers do drills with the infielders because they are infielders. I like them to play another position. Everyone worries about pitchers getting hurt doing this, but those pitchers who can field a position are a real asset. We have them do everything the other infielders do. They learn to dive. They do the pickups and short hops. They practice the backhand. And all of this increases their comfort as a defensive player, but also as an athlete. It solidifies your infield, and it helps them in every part of their game to learn to be aggressive rather than passive.

—Teresa Wilson

their fielding and hitting skills as well as working on their pitching, some pitchers like to make pitching practice an every-other-day routine. One day they are working almost exclusively on developing their speed and movement, but the next day they are doing fielding and hitting drills with the rest of the team. If there are several pitchers on your team, you can stagger who is "on" and who is "off" so there will always be a pitcher available to throw to the batters.

TEAMWORK

The pitcher is in the most influential position on the field; however, to achieve success, she still must have the support of her teammates. The offense has to supply runs to win, and the catcher, infielders, and outfielders have to catch and throw the ball flawlessly. There are times when the hitters will struggle at the plate and the fielders will make mistakes in the field. Times such as these require patience and understanding from the pitcher. Nobody likes to play behind a pitcher who is not appreciative of her teammates. Remember: On days when your pitches are getting hit hard, you will need your teammates.

DRILL TIME

THE FIELDING PITCHER

A great drill to help you work on your reaction time is a two-ball drill with your catcher and another person, a thrower, who stands next to the catcher. As you pitch, this thrower tosses a ball out to you before your pitch even gets to the catcher. You have to field this ball, which then becomes the next ball you pitch. The catcher hands the one you have pitched to the thrower.

FIRST BASEMAN DRILL

There will be situations where the pitcher needs to cover first base on ground balls. Any time the first baseman is playing back near the base and fields a ball to her right, the pitcher must quickly break for first base.

Have a coach or teammate hit groundballs toward the hole between first and second base. The pitcher runs from the mound to first base. As she approaches the bag, the first baseman leads her with an underhand toss. The pitcher catches the ball and tags the inside of first base.

Repeat this several times. It takes practice to get comfortable with the timing of the throw. Remember to touch the inside of first base and push off toward the infield. This will avoid any collision with the runner.

The pitcher may be the center of attention on the field but without those other eight fielders she's nothing. Don't forget to acknowledge your teammates for their good play behind you.

12

IV

PHYSICAL FITNESS

CONDITIONING YOUR BODY

To effectively run the bases, you've got to be in good condition.

Y ou want to be the best. You've worked hard on your hitting, fielding, and throwing, and your improvement as a softball player is visible to everyone. Have you maximized your potential? Not yet. There's one big element of the game left; one that can set you apart from your peers: Conditioning.

You swing the bat. Crack. It's a bullet to right-center. The center fielder dives for it, but it slides past her glove. The right fielder is sprinting over to back her up, but by this time you are rounding second. Your hit just might turn this into a home run. You approach third, and the coach is waving you in. But what's happening to you? You cannot get enough air. You are gasping for breath. Who knew you would ever have to run this far? You are out at the plate.

As infrequent as they are, inside-the-park home runs do happen, as do triples. When you train for a sport, you want to train for every possibility. A well-conditioned player has more energy, is more mentally alert, and possesses greater self-confidence than a player in average or below-average physical condition. Your body is like a car: It needs regular maintenance and care to perform at peak efficiency.

In softball you have primarily short sprints, with a few endurance tests (more if you are a pitcher). How do you set up your conditioning schedule to reflect this? Do you want a lot of long-

Building speed and endurance may allow you to turn a long single into an extra-base hit.

distance running? Probably not, although you do want to make sure you can make it around the bases, just in case that inside-the-park home run does present itself. Because that is a small part of the game, make it a small part of your training. The bulk of your conditioning training should be dedicated to short-burst exercises, because that is what you do in a game. As Marc Hill, a strength and conditioning coach for Arizona, says, "Just be sure to analyze the sport and train for it properly."

ANAEROBIC TRAINING

Anaerobic activity is defined as work the muscles do, in part, without air. In other words, it is activity performed at a level that is more intense than the body's oxygen-delivering system can keep up with. Think of the sprinting you do in every game. You have a twenty-yard sprint to a base, a twenty-yard sprint to get underneath the Texas leaguer, a forty-yard sprint to retrieve the ball that shot through the gap, etc. Because softball running is made up primarily of these short bursts of speed, anaerobic conditioning is the most important conditioning you can do. There are a variety of ways in which you can achieve this, but sprinting is the best, because that is what you will be doing in the game.

> The best thing a young player can do is to work on her range and do some strength and conditioning. But the reality is that most kids don't do that until they get to college.
>
> —Cindy Cohen, head coach, Princeton University

GOOD RUNNING FORM

Some people are natural runners; others are not. You may feel that you are in the latter category, but that does not mean that your running style cannot be improved. Working on good form and developing strong leg muscles through weight training can make you faster. In fact, you should consider running a skill and should work at it just as you would any other softball skill.

To start, stand tall. Get your head, shoulders, and chest all up in good posture form. Relax your arms, hands, and fingers. Tension will ruin your form and slow you down. Keep your eyes focused forward, not down. Keep your abdominals tight and your back flat. As you begin to run, lean forward slightly, still maintaining your good posture.

Now it is time to focus on the moving parts. Remember: Your goal is to go forward. With that in mind, you want to make sure that all your body parts are heading in that direction. Think of your legs as pistons, and drive them into the ground. Keep your knees high, but do not let your toes get in front of your knees. Stay up on the balls of your feet, and as your front leg moves to the back, get that heel up high. The higher it is, the more force it is going to have when it comes down again and pushes off the ground. When it hits the ground, it should then be almost fully extended.

Your arms are part of the sprint, too. Make a loose fist with your fingers and thumb, palms facing in, toward each other. Your elbows should be slightly bent, and your shoulders should be relaxed. The movement comes from the shoulders and is a back-and-forth motion, not a side-to-side one. Remember: All motion is

CONDITIONING DRILL

Following are three practice drills that will help players hone particular softball skills while improving their conditioning.

- *Foul-line-to-foul-line fly balls.* Players start on the left-field line. The players begin a sprint toward center field, and the coach hits a fly ball that the player must catch and throw to second base. The player then moves to a position in center field. The drill is repeated as the player sprints toward the right-field line to catch a fly ball and then throw to second base. After all the players reach the right-field line, they turn and repeat the drill, moving back toward the left-field line.

- *Wide-receiver fly balls.* The players line up along the right-field foul line. One by one, each player hands the coach a ball and then sprints toward center field. The coach throws the ball over the player's head. and each must sprint to the ball and catch it, just as a wide receiver would receive a pass from the quarterback.

- *Pickup drill.* Players are divided into two-girl teams. One girl kneels on one knee with two balls. The other girl stands in the ready position ten feet away. A ball is rolled to one side of the fielder, who fields it, tosses it back to her teammate, and laterally shuffles in the opposite direction to field the next ball. After twenty-five repetitions the girls change positions.

Practice proper form running every day. To develop a sense for what each body part needs to do, start out running in place.

toward the target. The lateral arm motion is a common running mistake that just expends energy without propelling you forward. If you are having trouble with this, think of leading backward with your elbow, even though the shoulder is doing the work. If you are still having trouble, get someone to videotape you. Once you see what you are doing, it is easier to make the necessary adjustments.

SPRINT WORKOUTS

Now that you have learned how to sprint, it is time to put your body to work. The easiest way to practice sprinting is with straight sprints, of course. You should do one set of straight sprints every day, in addition to the other conditioning you will do. Mix up the length of the sprints each day, however. For instance, one day you do twenty-yard sprints, and the next day you do hundred-yard sprints. You may want to repeat the shorter sprints six or eight times. For the longer ones, probably four repetitions are sufficient.

Another way to practice your sprinting is to tie it in with baserunning. Sprint to second as if you have hit a double, making sure you round first correctly. Rest for twenty seconds, and then sprint home. You can even practice sliding as well.

Sprinting against a fence or a wall is also good training. Lean at an angle against it, and push off, lifting those knees as high as you can. This is really something you can do anywhere, so you can sneak in a little sprint training when no one is looking.

This is a great drill that helps develop explosive movement. Lie down on your stomach with your hands up by your shoulders, palms to the ground. When your coach gives the signal, get your legs under you as quickly as possible and sprint forward about 30 yards.

CIRCUITS

Coaches love circuits. They keep the players busy, and nothing beats them for getting into shape. Nearly every coach in every sport has used them at one time or another. You do not have to have a coach to work out on a circuit, however. Setting one up yourself is easy, although it does help to have a partner.

Essentially, a circuit is a series of stations, each with a different activity, or series of activities. Each activity will last thirty seconds to one minute (depending on your level of conditioning), after which you will rest for an equal amount of time. The key to successful circuit training is to make sure you are using good form. If you find yourself getting sloppy because of fatigue, reduce the time spent at each station.

Working out with a partner is best, because one player can rest while the other is being conditioned. If you are alone, you'll just have to be creative about keeping an eye on the clock and making sure your form doesn't suffer. Here are a couple of sample circuits:

CIRCUIT 1

In this circuit you improve your anaerobic capacity, strengthen softball-appropriate muscles, and hone your coordination. Spend thirty to sixty seconds at each station, depending on your level of fitness.

1 Jump rope

2 Set up a five-yard square. Sprint on one side, shuffle on the next, sprint on the third, shuffle on the fourth, etc.

3 Place your glove on the ground and jump forward and backward over it.

4 Do push-ups.

Mountain climbers isolate the legs and help develop quickness and strength.

5 Lie on your stomach. On the whistle, get up and run as fast as you can.

6 Do sit-ups.

7 Mark a large X on the ground. Start on one top point of the X. Leap to the middle, then to the far bottom point. Leap over to the other bottom point. Go back to the middle, the last remaining point, and begin again.

8 Do mountain climbing (your hands are on the ground, and your feet are sprinting in place out behind you).

BEGINNER'S TIP

Improved reaction time can help you become a better baserunner and fielder. Here are some exercises that will improve your reaction time and better your conditioning, too.

1. Do a lateral shuffle, with the coach blowing a whistle to change your direction every few seconds.

2. Do the carioca (also called the grapevine). Alternate crossover steps as you move laterally. First the left leg crosses over behind the right, then it crosses over in front of the right. To move in the opposite direction, the right leg crosses alternately in front of and behind the left leg. Again, a coach should blow a whistle to have you change directions.

3. Sit down. Throw the ball in the air. Stand up and catch it. Sit down and repeat.

4. Lie on your back. On the whistle, get up and run.

5. Start in a three-point stance (two feet and one hand touching the ground) in front of second base, dive into the base, get up, and run to third.

This is a fun drill that helps improve speed, agility, strength, and hand-eye coordination. Sit on the ground with your legs bent in toward your midsection. Toss the ball up about 10 feet in the air. Stand up as fast as you can and catch the ball above your head. If you're having trouble standing up in time to catch the ball, throw it 15 feet in the air

CIRCUIT 2

In this circuit you work on sprint training. These sprints all begin at home plate and end at first base. When you reach first base, walk back to home plate and begin the next one.

1. Jog halfway, and sprint to first.

2. Jog halfway, pump your arms hard while running in place, and sprint to first.

3. Jog halfway, do tuck jumps (bring your arms to your side and jump up and down in place), and sprint to first.

4. Skip a third, lunge-walk a third (take giant steps, bringing your upper body over your thigh on each step), and sprint to first.

5. Jog halfway, work high knees in place, and sprint to first.

6. Jog, sprint, jog, and sprint.

7. Jog a third, run backward a third, and sprint.

8. Sprint halfway, stop but keep your feet moving in place, and sprint it out.

AEROBIC TRAINING

Aerobic (*aero* is the Latin word meaning "air") activity means that the oxygen is inhaled by the lungs, passed through the bloodstream and carried to the working muscles, all at a rate sufficient to keep up with the muscles' demand for air. After all the sprint training and circuit work, your body is going to be begging for something easy, like a long-distance run. And that is not a joke. Even though your aerobic needs are few in softball, any athletic activity can benefit from a good aerobic base. Just because that inside-the-park home run is rare does not mean it is okay to be sucking wind as you round third base. You want to have the ability to stretch that double into a triple.

Put on those jogging shoes and hit the track. Running is an excellent way to improve your aerobic capacity. As a softball player, you—pitchers excepted—will not want to waste time doing a lengthy cross-country run. Something shorter is more sport-appropriate. Rather than running a 10K regularly, work on shorter distances at faster speeds.

A mile is a good distance for softball. Time yourself as you run it, then work on getting a faster time. Nine minutes is a good time; eight is better. Most people will probably find themselves somewhere in between. Running a fast mile will improve your aerobic conditioning and build up your quadriceps muscles (the big muscles at the front of your thighs), which are used in sprinting. Strong leg muscles also build up the power base that is so crucial in hitting. You can also build up these muscles by bike-riding.

If you are a pitcher, you should include aerobic workouts that are more demanding. You are nearly always in motion, and if you want to last seven innings, you had better be in good shape. Do those two- to three-mile runs regularly, instead of the faster one-mile run, and occasionally push yourself for a five-mile run.

Although softball does not seem like an endurance sport, hard work under the sun can be draining. Get your body into shape well before the season starts, and you won't regret it.

DRILL TIME

RELAY RACE

Divide the players into two teams. Station half of each team at each foul pole. Have the players race to the opposite foul pole and touch one of their teammates, who returns to the other foul pole. Pitchers must run twice.

END-OF-INNING RUN

Conditioning during the season can be done while you are working on other skills. A fun way to do this is to set up players in their defensive positions and give them a two-out scenario, with runners on base. Hit the ball and have them try to get the runners out. If they get an out, everyone sprints off the field to the dugout and then sprints back into position for another play.

STRENGTH TRAINING

Strong muscles help prevent injury, and strong muscles improve performance. Strength training will help you in every aspect of your game: hitting, throwing, sprinting, etc. The stronger you are, the more power you can put into your swing, your throw, or your drive as you run the bases.

A stronger player is a better player.

Table 1 describes the different muscles that are used in softball and some exercises that help strengthen them. Many of the exercises involve the use of free weights or weight equipment, but some of the best strength-training exercises, such as lunges or sit-ups, can be done anywhere. The beauty of these exercises is that they often work several muscles at once.

Before entering a strength-training program, understand that a program will only benefit you if you're committed. Building muscles and improving strength takes time and dedication. It does not happen overnight. In fact, it's very possible that you will go through a period of soreness before feeling stronger. The only way to make the soreness and hard work pay off is to maintain a regimented schedule over several weeks or months.

The most common mistake young athletes make when they begin strength training is giving up on it prematurely. Because they don't notice immediate results, they feel as if they are not gaining anything from their workouts. Do not fall victim to being

2

impatient. Rome was not built in a day so don't expect your physique to be either. Continue to work hard.

Adding strength to your physique will allow you to hit the ball harder and farther.

DEVELOPING YOUR TRAINING PROGRAM

Just like finding a batting stance, you have to find a workout program and schedule that feels comfortable to you. Do not assume that your personal workout should be identical to your teammate's. Every girl is different. There are girls who develop physical maturity at an earlier stage in their life, some are stronger or weaker due to their genetics, and others may have prior experience in strength-training. Design your workout so it's specific to your needs. Modeling it after another teammate's can be nonproductive and possibly dangerous.

To devise a training program, you should solicit advice from two main sources. First, talk with your coach and identify the areas he or she feels you need to improve. Your coach may tell that you need more strength in your legs or forearms. Although the ultimate goal is to increase the strength throughout your entire body, there are specific muscles that you need to address when playing softball.

The second person you should visit is a fitness instructor or strength and conditioning coach. If you do not have access to a

WEIGHT-TRAINING WARMING

Your body needs to have developed to almost full adult size before you begin a weight-training program. Most girls are ready for this in high school, but younger girls should concentrate on improving their skills rather than increasing their muscle mass. Muscle workouts while the body is still growing can cause permanent damage to ligaments and tendons.

Push-ups and sit-ups are two simple exercises that will increase strength in your upper body and mid-section.

specialist, ask your physical education teacher at school. They are qualified to give basic guidance and advice on physical conditioning. Tell them what you hope to accomplish, the time period you have available, and the equipment you have access to. They can help you design a program that is suitable to your needs.

STRENGTHENING EXERCISES

A good weight workout uses a combination of free weights, weight machines, and strength exercises. The most popular weight machines, such as Nautilus, tell you exactly which muscle you are working. Unfortunately, everyone does not have access to the best equipment. If you do not have access to a training room, you still can do strength exercises. Following is a list of many common strength-building exercises for which you don't need access to weight-training equipment.

❶ **Push-ups** (chest, deltoids, triceps). Lie face down on the floor with your hands, palm down, just outside your shoulders. Your legs and body should be straight. Press upward, lifting your body off the ground until your elbows are fully extended. Now, with your back straight and your eyes forward, lower yourself until you chest brushes the floor, extend your arms and repeat the motion.

Strength conditioning is not just simply for the benefit of getting big and strong, but also for being able to play at the highest level possible with as few injuries as possible.

—Marc Hill, strength and conditioning coach, University of Arizona

❷ Isometric lats (upper back, shoulders). Isometrics exercise pits one muscle against another or against an immovable object in a strong but motionless flexing or contracting. To work the shoulder area, lift your arms over your head and cross your wrists, making fists with your hands. Contract (tighten) the muscles in your arms, shoulders, and upper body. Pull down and then move back up, holding the contraction.

❸ Bench-rowing (deltoids). Place your right knee and right arm on a bench (or coffee table). Place a dumbbell (or a small bag filled with cans or books or something heavy) on the floor. Reach down with your left arm and pull the weight straight up. Switch sides and repeat the exercise.

❹ Reeling (arm muscles, including wrists and forearms). Tie a three- or four-foot string to a weight and then tie the other end to a broomstick or softball bat. Hold the stick or bat out in front of you, with your palms facing down, and reel the weight up by turning the stick until all the string is wrapped around it. Repeat holding the stick palms up and reeling again.

❺ Sit-ups (abdominal muscles). Lie on your back with your legs bent, feet flat on the floor. Place your hands loosely behind your head. Lift your upper body off the floor a few inches, making sure you exhale as you do this. Hold this position for a count of "3." Inhale as you go back down.

❻ Abdominal twists (stomach and side muscles). Follow the same instructions as for sit-ups, but when your upper body is off the floor, rotate your upper body first to one side, then back to the center, then to the other side, and then finally back down to rest.

❼ Calf-raises (calf muscles). Stand with both feet on the ground. Raise up onto your toes, hold for a few seconds, and then slowly return your heels to the floor.

❽ Wall-sits (quadriceps). Press your back up against the wall and slide down into a sitting position, as though you were sitting in a chair. Your thighs should be parallel with the floor, and your feet flat on the ground. Slide back up the wall and repeat the movement several times.

❾ Step-ups (hamstrings, gluteus, quadriceps). Stand in front of a one-foot-high bench or in front of a set of stairs. Step up onto the bench (or the second step if you are using stairs). Bring your other foot up. Step down with one foot, then the other. Repeat the movement, alternating which leg you lead with.

⑩ **Lunges** (quadriceps, gluteus). Stand with your hands on your hips. Maintaining good posture, with your head up, facing forward, take a giant step with one leg, reaching out so your thigh is parallel to the ground. Do not let your front knee extend beyond the front of your foot. Return to standing and repeat with the other leg.

⑪ **Side lunges** (hips, gluteus). Begin as you would for a lunge, but instead of stepping forward, step sideways, while your trunk remains facing forward. Again, make sure that your knee does not extend beyond the front of your foot. Return to the standing position, and repeat the movement in the other direction.

⑫ **Squats** (hamstrings, quadriceps, gluteus). Stand with your hands on your hips, feet shoulder width apart. Maintaining good posture, bend your knees, keeping your feet in place. Do not let your knees extend beyond the front of your feet. Return to standing position.

TABLE 1—MUSCLE CHART

MUSCLE	REASONS	EXERCISES
Quadriceps (front of thigh)	Quickness Leg power Base of support Transfer of weight	Squats Lunges
Hamstring (back of thigh)	Leg drive Power Speed	Squats Leg curls
Gluteus (rear end)	Power pack for hitting and throwing	Squats Lunges
Abdominals (stomach) and lower back	Link of power Fatigue fighter Rotational moves	Sit-ups Hypers
Pectorals (chest)	Stabilize the shoulder Angle of the throwing arm	Bench press Incline press
Deltoids (shoulder)	Throwing follow-through Overhead movements	Shoulder routine
Triceps (back of upper arm)	Pull through when hitting Throwing accelerator	Lying extensions Press-downs Pressing motions
Hips	Rotational power for hitting	Hammer rotations Squats Lunges

WORKOUTS

For each exercise you should work the same muscle for a number of repetitions. For example, do six lunges with each leg, then rest and do six more. This is what is known as a set. After the four sets, move on to another exercise, involving different muscles. Two or three sets of six to twelve repetitions for each exercise is a good workout for anyone from beginner on up. If you are in the weight room, start with lighter weights. After a comfortable first set, you can either increase the weight or increase the number of repetitions. In general, a beginning weight trainer should work out for about twenty minutes, whereas a more advanced weight trainer should be working her muscles for about an hour.

Weight training should not be done every day. When you lift weights, your muscles become tired and worn, and they need time to recover. Vary your conditioning by running one day and weight training the next. It is also wise to alternate among muscle groups when weight training. Work on your legs one day, you arms and shoulders the next time, then your chest and back regions. Table 2 shows a sample workout for a week.

You want to make sure that you train your whole body, so your body stays balanced. For example, when you are hitting, a number of muscles are working together to swing the bat. You do not want to overstrain certain muscles so they cause an imbalance in your swing. Conversely, you do not want your swing to suffer because you have neglected a muscle group.

Ideally, all these strength workouts should be done in the off-season. Think about what in-season weight training would do to your body. Weight training the day before the game does not give your body time to recover. You can condition during the season without weight training.

Lunges, which assist in developing power in the quadriceps and gluteus regions, can be performed in your backyard.

TABLE 2—SAMPLE OFF-SEASON WORKOUT WEEK

MONDAY

Squats	4 sets of 6 repetitions
Step-ups	3 sets of 12 repetitions
Calves	3 sets of 12 repetitions
Push-ups	4 sets of 6 repetitions
Isometric lats	4 sets of 6 repetitions
Tricep pulls	3 sets of 8 repetitions
Bicep curls	3 sets of 8 repetitions
Shoulder press	3 sets of 8 repetitions
Pull-ups	4 sets of 2 repetitions
Sit-ups	4 sets of 50 repetitions

TUESDAY

Conditioning circuits

WEDNESDAY

Leg curls	4 sets of 6 repetitions
Calves	3 sets of 12 repetitions
Dumbbell rowing	4 sets of 6 repetitions
Tricep pushdown	3 sets of 8 repetitions
Shoulder raises	3 sets of 12 repetitions
Situps	3 sets of 20 repetition

THURSDAY

Three mile run

FRIDAY

Squats	3 sets of 6 repetitions
Angle lunges	3 sets of 12 repetitions
Bench presses	3 sets of 8 repetitions
Pull-down for back	3 sets of 6 repetitions
Hammer curls	3 sets of 8 repetitions
Crunches	2 sets of 50 repetitions
Abdominal twists	2 sets of 50 repetitions

SATURDAY

Sprintwork

SUNDAY

Rest

The best way to train all of the muscles used to hit is to swing the bat. Whether it be off of a tee, taking soft toss (6), dry swinging, or during batting practice, swinging the bat over and over increases power and bat speed.

DRILL TIME

THE READY-POSITION ROLL

Softball players have to be in the ready position at the start of every pitch. This can be awfully tiring on the quad muscles, so these need to be especially strong. The best way to train for this ready-position crouch is to train in it. Two players face each other in the ready position, about five to ten feet apart, depending on the skill level. Player A has the ball. She rolls it to the right, and Player B fields it and rolls it back to Player A's right. She fields it and rolls it back to Player B's left, and so on, for whatever amount of time seems appropriate for their skill and conditioning level. The players should remain in the ready position for the entire drill. If the drill gets too easy, a second ball can be introduced.

If we're playing Tuesday, Thursday, Saturday, and Sunday, trying to fit in recovery days after strength training is impossible. We just try to get as strong as we can before the season starts and then do our best to maintain it.

—Tricia Carrol, head coach, Rider University

ENHANCING YOUR FLEXIBILITY

Many young athletes become complacent about stretching their muscles. They haven't pulled a muscle yet, they are fairly limber, and frankly, the flexibility training is boring. If this sounds like you, you are making a big mistake. An athlete with flexible muscles is not only less likely to get hurt, but also she will become a better athlete by increasing her range of motion.

Softball uses the entire body, so the entire body must be stretched. No matter which muscle is being targeted, there are a few simple rules to follow.

Flexibility improves performance and helps avoid injuries.

❶ Stretch only after warming up your muscles; they are more resilient then.

❷ Never bounce.

❸ Hold the stretch for fifteen to twenty seconds.

❹ As you exhale, try to extend your reach, holding for another ten seconds.

Stretching is a must before any high-intensity activity. Warm up your muscles with a light workout—a slow jog, for example—and then move into your stretching routine. When you are finished with your activity, you need to stretch again before your muscles cool down. You should also stretch your muscles after any strength training. In fact, stretching can be done anywhere, as long as the muscles are warm.

Here is a list of basic stretches for all the main muscles in your body. Ideally you want to hold each stretch until you feel the muscle start to relax. Then you lengthen the stretch until you feel the resistance again. The stretches listed here start with the ankles and work their way up the body to the head. It is a good idea to stretch bottom to top or top to bottom, because it helps you track which muscles you have already targeted.

Use the ankle stretch shown in to avoid twisting an ankle (2). To help stretch your hamstrings (3), cross one leg over the other, bend down and try to touch your toes. If you can't reach your toes, go down as far as you can without bending at the knees.

STRETCHING EXERCISES

ANKLE

In softball, the ankle is not as vulnerable as it is in sports such as basketball or soccer, but you never know when you will run across a poorly maintained field with a small hole just waiting to grab your foot. No one wants a season ended by a nasty sprain, so stretch your ankles every day. This stretch is simple: Lift your foot off the ground, point your toe, flex your foot forward and back, and make circles with your toe as you rotate the ankle joint. Spend the same amount of time on each ankle.

CALF AND ACHILLES TENDON

Two stretches target this area. If you have a wall or a fence nearby, lean against it at about a forty-five-degree angle. Stretch

Strength is wasted if you are not flexible.
—Marc Hill, strength and conditioning coach, University of Arizona

Take the extra time to stretch out your hamstrings. Pulling or even straining a hamstring can keep you from playing for a lengthy period of time.

one leg out behind you as far as it can go while still keeping the heel on the ground. Hold the stretch, then switch legs.

Lean against the wall or fence, face first at a forty-five-degree angle. Stretch one leg out behind you with the toe pointing away from you. Keep your other heel firmly on the ground. Hold the stretch and switch legs.

If you do not have a wall or a fence, you can do this stretch on the ground. Position yourself in the push-up position. Bring one leg forward to support your body and press the heel of the other leg to the ground. Hold the stretch, then switch legs.

HAMSTRING

The hamstring is the large muscle in the back of your thigh. Here are two stretches for the hamstring. The first stretch is your basic toe touch, with a twist. In a standing position, cross one leg over the other, bend down, and touch your toes. Try to keep your legs as straight as possible without locking your knees. Cross the other leg over and repeat.

The second hamstring stretch is done lying on your back. While keeping one leg straight, pull the knee of the other leg to your chest. Hold it for ten seconds and relax. Repeat with the opposite leg.

QUADRICEPS

The quadriceps muscle is the large muscle in the front of your thigh. This muscle is best stretched while standing. Bend the lower half of one leg, bringing your heel up toward your rear end, then grab your ankle with your hand and pull up on the ankle until you feel the stretch in the quadriceps muscle. Hold and then switch to the other leg.

If you have trouble maintaining balance in this position, you can hold on to a partner's shoulder or a wall, fence, etc. If you are out in the middle of the field, you can focus your eyes on something on the ground about five or six feet in front of you. This helps you stay upright.

HIP

There are two good hip-stretching exercises. The first is called the pretzel, primarily because you position your legs like a pretzel to isolate the right spot. This stretch is done seated on the ground. First extend your right leg. Then place your left foot on the ground next to your right knee. Now place your right elbow on the left side of the left knee. This should twist your body enough so you feel a stretch in the left hip. Then switch and do the right hip.

The second stretch is called the hip roll. Lie on your back and bend both knees, keeping your feet on the ground. To stretch your right hip, roll both knees to the left and both arms to the right. To stretch the left hip, roll both knees to the right and both arms to the left.

This exercise stretches out the quadriceps muscle. While standing on one leg, grab the ankle of the leg you're stretching and pull it up toward your rear end. Hold it for ten seconds and then switch legs.

GROIN

The best stretch for the groin muscle is something called the butterfly stretch. Sit on the ground. Place the soles of your feet together so your legs are bent and your knees are sticking out like butterfly wings. Use your elbows to push your knees down to the ground. If you do not feel the stretch in the groin at this point, try leaning forward.

LOWER BACK

Lie on your back, knees bent, feet on the ground. Bring one knee up to your chest and hold it. Put that leg back on the ground and bring the other one up to your chest. Then bring both legs up to your chest. Make sure you pull them in tightly so you can really

All three of these exercises are used to stretch body parts above your legs. (6) is the side stretch which helps loosen up the waist. (7) illustrates a chest stretch which limbers up the pectoral region. (8) is an example of a forearm stretch. The forearm muscles are major contributors to hitting and throwing so make sure they are loose for competition.

feel the stretch in your lower back. This exercise also stretches the hamstring muscle.

WAIST

To stretch your waist, start in a standing position. Raise one arm up and then lean and stretch toward the opposite arm. You should feel the stretch up and down the side of your body. Switch arms and lean the other way.

TORSO

You will need a wall or a fence to do the stretch called the torso twist. Stand perpendicular to the wall and extend your arm out to meet it. Then reach your other arm around to that hand without changing the position of your feet. Turn, face the other way, and do the other side.

CHEST

Stand up for this one. Put your arms behind your back and clasp your hands. Then raise your arms as much as you can, keeping your hands clasped.

FOREARM

The forearm muscle is probably the most important muscle for a hitter because the forearms and the wrists are providing the snap to the swing. Alway stretch your forearm muscles.

You can do this one standing or sitting. Extend one arm out in front of you, with the palm facing the ground. Then reach over with the other hand and pull the fingers on the extended hand toward the ground. Switch arms and repeat the exercise.

TRICEPS

The triceps is the muscle in the back of your upper arm, opposite the biceps muscle. To stretch the triceps, raise your right arm over your head. Then bend that arm at the elbow and let the right hand drop down to the back. With the left hand, pull that right elbow toward the back as well. Switch arms and repeat the exercise.

Stretch out the triceps by bending one arm behind your head and pulling on the elbow with your opposite arm (9). The shoulders are also very valuable to softball players so loosen them up by grabbing your hand and pulling it across your chest (10).

SHOULDER

Stretching the shoulder is crucial for anyone who is going to be throwing the ball, which means everyone. There are two good stretches for the shoulder, both of which are done standing up. For the first stretch, extend an arm up in the air. Without bending your torso, stretch your arm as far as possible toward the opposite shoulder. You can even pull it with the other arm if you need to.

The second stretch comes across your body. Extend the arm straight out in front of you and then use your other arm to pull your arm across your chest, again without twisting your body.

You do not have to stretch every muscle every day, but it is a good habit to get into. Just remember: All this stretching should be done on warm muscles, and it should be done both before and after your workout.

INDEX